Lincoln

Freedom Fighter

Lincoln

Freedom Fighter

A Biography of Abraham Lincoln

J.R. MacGregor

Lincoln - Freedom Fighter

Copyright © 2021 JR MacGregor

All rights reserved. No portion of this book may be reproduced, stored in a retrieval system, or transmitted in any form or by any means – electronic, mechanical, photocopy, recording, scanning, or other – except for brief quotations in critical reviews or articles, without prior written permission of the publisher.

Published by CAC Publishing LLC

ISBN 978-1-950010-48-6 paperback

ISBN 978-1-950010-47-9 eBook

Table of Contents

Introduction 8

Chapter 1 - Foundations in American History 13

Chapter 2 - E Pluribus Unum 38

Chapter 3 - Phases of Life 43

Chapter 4 - Thomas Lincoln 53

Chapter 5 - Development 65

Chapter 6 - Young Adulthood 76

Chapter 7 - Spreading His Wings 84

Chapter 8 - First True Love 102

Chapter 9 - State Legislator 112

Chapter 10 - Marriage and Life After 125

Chapter 11 - Lincoln's Angels & Demons 159

Chapter 12 - Spiritual Center 177

Chapter 13 - National Politics 198

Chapter 14 - Politician 214

Chapter 15 - Electoral Math 229

Chapter 16 - The Presidency 237

Chapter 17 - Lincoln's War 261

Chapter 18 - Second Term 264

Chapter 19 - John Wilkes Booth 273

Chapter 20 - Last Act 279

Conclusion 282

Introduction

"I believe this Government cannot endure, permanently half slave and half free. I do not expect the Union to be dissolved--I do not expect the house to fall--but I do expect it will cease to be divided."

Abraham Lincoln, June 16, 1858

The presidency is more than just an office created by the force of the Articles of the U.S. Constitution. It is the hill upon which men of charisma ascend to lead a nation of diversity and to inspire an entire generation. Not all who aspire to the office, though, have the God-given resources to be successful. Even fewer stand the time in accomplishing a positive change so profound that he leaves the annals of history and enters the pantheon of legends. Abraham Lincoln was such a legend but not because he freed the slaves or fought the only civil war to unfold within these shores.

Lincoln is a legend because he made manifest the motto of the United States—*E Pluribus Unum*, from many, one. The joining of people and states was the goal of the unification that took years to articulate in a document, debate at conventions, and argue about at homes.

Before Lincoln, the country was splintered. It may have been under one national flag, but it was a collection of different cultures. It was still referred to as "these united states" instead of "this United States."

A president is not limited to the office that is given power by the Constitution. He is also the man who brings the country together by virtue of how he gets into office. The president is the only officeholder that every citizen has a hand in electing. Each citizen lends him an ear when he speaks, each citizen resonates when he tolls, and ignites when he lights the flames. Only the president can bring a country together and make the words *"that all men are created equal, that they are endowed by their Creator with certain unalienable rights, that among these are life, liberty and the pursuit of happiness"* manifest.

Lincoln embodied the presidency unlike many of the officeholders who had been elected to that office before him or since. Each man can only be fairly judged by how he handles the events that are presented to him during his presidency. So, while it is unfair to force another president into the same criteria one would judge someone like George Washington or FDR, Abraham Lincoln stood solitary in his accomplishments and lasting. You can't expect every president to win a war while in office or oversee the reunification of a country. Instead, you have to observe the factors he brought to the table and extrapolate his contributions from the good that came from his time.

In doing that, encapsulating Lincoln needs to be a lifetime endeavor that is spread across numerous books. To do it in just one requires just the salient points and for those points to be placed in context. That context comes in the form of a rags-to-riches story except it does not refer to wealth but to opportunity and accomplishment. Moving slowly but resolutely the way he did, from the backwater of zero opportunity to the capital of a vibrant democracy, is nothing short of inspired. Add to that, observing and empathizing with the challenges he faced inside elevated his accomplishments that were already stratospheric in its continuation to the way we live our lives today.

It turns out that it was his inner rotten demons that made his outer better angles take flight. There was a darkness within Lincoln that would have crushed most men. It is not the demons that deserve attention; it is the angels he summoned to lift him out of the depths and raise him to the heavens.

Depression colored him inside but never stained his soul. He used the power and stamina of his mind to beat back the negative thoughts that filled his head. The story of the life that was handed to him was the typical frontier story. It was filled with anecdotes of hard work, fears of uncertain days ahead, visions of self-sufficient acts, tears from the loss of loved ones, and heroic battles with the elements.

Depression was not a unique issue among frontiersmen back then. It was also a prevalent condition that afflicted immigrants who had fled their country in fear of hardship and landed in a country that was nothing but wilderness and uncertainty. Depression had even touched Lincoln's father, which caused him to act and perform differently from most other men. It was a cause of heartache for young Lincoln, who eventually thought it better to leave his father's side and make it on his own.

All this—the life that he lived as a child, a son, a brother, and a frontiersman—happened on the backdrop of a new nation that was a nation in name only until he came along and made it a nation in spirit as well.

Chapter 1 - Foundations in American History

"The best way to predict your future is to create it."

Abraham Lincoln, Sixteenth President of the United States

On February 12, 1809, the day President Lincoln was born, the United States of America numbered only seventeen states: Rhode Island, Vermont, Connecticut, New York, Pennsylvania, Delaware, Maryland, Virginia, Ohio, Kentucky, Tennessee, New Jersey, North Carolina, South Carolina, and Georgia.

All were located east of the Mississippi River.

Indiana Territory, Louisiana Territory, and Orleans Territory were located west of the Mississippi River and would not become states until later. This state of things made for a very different country during a very different period of time.

The banding together of a coalition of colonies to fend off King George and his taxation without representation had only happened a mere three decades before. The U.S. Constitution had only been in effect for twenty-two years, superseding the law of individual states and giving rise to the Office of the President, Congress, and the Supreme Court, which was the arbiter of conflict in laws between the states and the federal Constitution, and now they felt more that they were begrudgingly stuck with each other—instead of being stronger—united.

The states were delineated by more than just lines drawn on a map. They were divided by geography in many places, by self-interest everywhere, and all were injected with the self-interest of politicians, who found strength in division rather that unification. One of the side effects democracies have to endure is the fear-mongering of us versus them by shortsighted politicians.

The Founding Fathers of the United States understood that local politics between competing localities would take on an us-versus-them shade and needed a mechanism to balance that. At the same time, they understood that no man can make the decision his neighbor would because each man occupies the well in his own shoes and can't possibly understand the predicament of his neighbor who made a decision differently from him.

The day Lincoln was born Thomas Jefferson was serving out the last few weeks of his term as president. The election of 1808, a few weeks earlier, had yielded president-elect James Madison, who would be sworn in a few weeks later on March 4 and see Jefferson return to Monticello.

The Honorable John Marshall was Chief Justice of the Supreme Court, which that same year as Lincoln's humble birth in the backwoods of Kentucky, had been part of a majority decision to enforce the supremacy of the court in matters of deciding the extent of states' rights versus federal power and jurisdiction. Half a century later it would become the one of the central thrusts that powered Lincoln's political ascendancy.

At a granular level, the issue of states' rights versus federal supremacy had been stewing. Each man's loyalty was resoundingly to his state and his community. This was significantly more so than it was to the new republic. Loyalty to something larger than what he could traverse easily was beyond the imagination of the average man, who would typically live out his entire life without leaving his county or his state.

Reasons for loyalty also went beyond this issue of affinity. They even included and probably more so the issue of self-preservation and self-importance. These issues were the main drivers of the democracy practiced in the states and the well from which politicians sent to the capital drank. These politicians and their politics were critical elements of stoking the discord of difference.

To the farmers and settlers, neighboring states may have been easier to fathom, but distant reaches were illusory and unworthy of the extra thought. Sitting on a farm in Hodgenville, Kentucky, in 1800 and thinking about Cambridge, Massachusetts, was like sitting in Wichita, Kansas, today and thinking about somewhere far away, such as Somalia. They certainly didn't feel like countrymen, and the locals from each jurisdiction had differing issues to focus on. America today with all the technology and communication still bears this out.

Asking someone to pledge his loyalty to something so illusory was a stretch, especially when it came at the cost of his livelihood or in opposition to his own needs, principles, and beliefs. This was magnified when self-serving politicians expounded issues of division when it suited them and their aspirations.

What is commonplace to us today—visiting distant reaches of the country—was alien then to those who lived their entire lives within a few square miles of where they were born and where they would eventually die. This caused a wildly different mind-set of what one could be loyal to or call his home. It took men with imagination, like that of Jefferson and Lincoln, to see that the individual states, united, would evolve and develop into something much greater than just the sum of its parts. Jefferson was fighting for it in his lifetime, and Lincoln achieved it in his.

Each man is made up of more than a solitary experience or a singular ideal. We are all a compendium of impressions and a conglomerate of desires. So, too, was Lincoln. His ideals and vision of the nation stretched beyond the borders of a state. Perhaps it was because he had traveled from one backwoods town to the the next, spent time on one farm, then the next, sailed on rivers, journeyed across plains, and saw the expanse of the country from the lakes in the North to the Gulf in the South and from the shores in the East to the plains in the West. He understood the scope of the country as something beyond just a few counties.

Being a collection of states instead of being one country meant having soft borders. These borders between states complicated matters. They weren't just random lines drawn on a map. They represented the extent to which laws of different states would have effect.

Being a country of laws meant that no one man had power over the land, and it meant that equity and equanimity were guaranteed by the laws that defined the lines of demarcation between the states. It was these laws that gave rise and imbued life into the land. For every grain of tangible sand that made up the land, there was an intangible dome of protection that was created by the laws men agreed upon and instituted.

America was, is, and always will be a land of laws, but these laws, while on one hand were designed to protect those in its jurisdiction, could sometimes prove to be in opposition to laws that were designed to protect those in neighboring jurisdictions.

That disparity did not do anything to draw the people in different states together; instead, it seemed there was a state-sponsored effort to divide the people. But there wasn't. There just wasn't enough understanding of the mechanisms of the new republic.

It was important, though, that each state legislated the necessary framework to be able to provide for that particular state's unique conditions. That had positive and negative consequences. Because people, their movement, and their activity patterns are fluid, they naturally oscillate back and forth across these intangible borders. They create relationships, cement transactions, and advance through life impervious to the waning of one set of laws and the waxing of another across state lines.

In theory, it may not have been that important, but in practice it was a major hindrance and a source of widespread frustration. The differing state laws would often work in concert and worked well to facilitate interaction, but one state's laws would often inconvenience the citizens of a neighboring state. Such places as neighboring New Jersey and New York that shared the waters in New York Harbor found this to be a difficult issue and gave rise to mischief.

In areas where these differing laws came into contention, the Constitution had foreseen some areas this could happen and relegated these areas to the federal government's jurisdiction. That was, in part, the idea of the Union. It was not only convenient to bring about economies of scale, but it was also practical to have an impartial foundation of legal structures to cover matters that may involve cross-border issues.

Only the Supreme Court was empowered to adjudicate whether a state's law was its own business or ceded to the federal government by virtue of the U.S. Constitution. Criminal behavior in one state or conducted across state lines, for instance, would be problematic without federal law and the Constitution. The construction of the Constitution was supposed to be the buffer that managed the competing laws across borders and contradictory laws that were legislated down the road.

One issue that grew precarious because of this structure in law and order was the regulation and institution of slavery. Some states allowed it;

some states did not. To the states that allowed slavery, they were the engine of growth, the root of wealth, and the bane of humanity. To the states that didn't, the question was split. Should they mind their own business or should they enforce their morals on the states that allowed slavery? The issues of states' rights and slavery were on a collision course. The issue of morality and wealth was also on a collision course. The issue of racism and religion was also at odds with each other and so were so many other matters that rose with the sun at the dawn of the American story.

The question had even been put to the framers of the Constitution during the Constitutional Convention more than thirty years before Lincoln was even born. The South knew very well that there was disagreement with the immoral acts of slavery and that they needed some kind of protection to be able to preserve their institution. Even Thomas Jefferson was pushed back when his original draft of the Declaration of Independence was first presented. Parts of it were rejected because of its antislavery tone, and the delegates were afraid that if they took those back to their respective colonies the support for it would evaporate, and the Second Continental Congress would not be able to pass the Declaration. Slavery has had a significant clout in the history of the United States.

In the South, where slavery was a major part of life, they had already tried to use the neighboring states in the North as a slave net. They wanted the Constitution to enforce their (the South's) laws in the North so that the slaves who did run north would be caught and sent back. The argument that they wanted a federal system to act as a policeman or a bounty hunter is more accurate than the South wanting to promote a centralized government over states' rights.

Lincoln could see through the South's facade. He understood that the issues they were talking about undoubtedly led back to the issue of slavery. The politicians of the South had a vested interest in the fraught state of affairs and the systemic racism that had become the vessel in which it not only affected the soul of the individual but also the godliness of a nation.

Racism in the South was not sparked by the racism of hatred. It was fueled by the racism of economics. To the target of racism, that distinction was lost. Dehumanizing abuse by any other name is still as painful, but the distinction serves to understand that the moral vacuum that existed back then was so overwhelming that it managed to blind Christian eyes into reading the Bible to mean that racism, slavery, and abuse were God's will. Lincoln rejected this interpretation to the fullest and initially rejected the Bible because of it as well.

To racists, what they knew to be right was traded for dollars and cents and then masked in arcane passages from the Bible. The wealth and livelihood of the South was predicated on the suppression of an entire race of people but was masked in and sanctioned by the righteousness of religion.

Lincoln would have none of it. He rejected the South's fake interpretation of the Constitution and their understanding of the intent of the framers and the Founding Fathers. He was intimately familiar with the writings of his favorite president, Jefferson, and the books that Jefferson himself had relied on to shape his own mind and thoughts on the matter. While Lincoln did not need to study Greek and Latin to drink from the same intellectual trough as Jefferson, he merely had to study Jefferson's words.

Looking within, Lincoln could no longer sit still and take what was happening in the political realm of his country and the moral well of the nation. Both were fraying at the seams and destroying the intent of the Founding Fathers from within. It has always been said that America cannot be destroyed but from within. In the twenty-first century, the world is witnessing such an attempt, but in the mid-nineteenth century, the self-serving nature of the Southern politicians who fed the flames of fear on behalf of the influential owner class in society was the catalyst of chaos.

To understand Lincoln, it is important to understand the South and the politics of deception that was practiced by the politicians.

Because of their actions, the issues of states' rights and slavery become intertwined, making the latter the proxy for the former.

It wasn't about slavery alone, and it was not about power in the South in isolation. Over the last two hundred years, the two had become two sides of the same issue. Slavery had become a billion-dollar industry, and scrapping that stain off the fabric of society boiled to such stratospheric contention that they melded into one and the same.

At the start, in the first fifty years, the conveniences of unity were outweighed by the differences in opinion and practice. England presented a greater threat to their freedom and to their wealth. The magnates of the South saw independence as the lesser of two evils and one they could wield to their will.

For the first hundred years, the slave-owning class had their way, but it seemed that the differences were growing more stark. Around the time Lincoln began voicing his concerns against slavery and a certain part of the Whigs had started to champion the abolition movement, the South had begun to ramp up their slave dependencies.

To understand the reason behind the upswing in slave ownership and dependency, it is necessary to think about the world holistically. The Industrial Revolution, especially the part of it that had to do with the mechanization of the textile mills in Lancashire, England, and Scotland, not to mention the ones in France and Germany, were starting to shift their dependence on the cotton coming from America's South. This move created significant competitive forces and enormous wealth in the Deep South. There was also competition from South India and other parts of Asia, but the American South had the benefits of lower cost, which contributed to the slave labor. Without slave labor, it would have been likely that they would have lost their cost-competitive position.

To keep slaves in the South, they also needed states in the North to help capture them when they managed to flee. Under the auspices of this ability to enact law and have it enforced beyond their own borders, the South initially tried to use the Constitution to its benefit at the cost of the slaves and the North.

To think that it was only slavery that sparked the highlight of Lincoln's career would be simplifying a critical juncture in American history and diminishing the toil and effort that went into addressing it. To say that it was the problem of balancing states' rights with central governing would be insufficient in capturing the full reason. Together, they come closer to the truth but still do not encapsulate the full extent of the stakes Lincoln had to contend with.

Slavery, as contentious and fraught as it was on its own, was also the vessel that held a compendium of other frustrations and aspirations of the South under one umbrella. Those differences included ideological chasms, cultural asymmetries, moral divergence, and even religious interpretations.

The issue of states' rights had evolved into a matter of sovereignty. The South took on an air of its own distinct from the "Yankees" in an effort to draw the lines of culture, heritage, and governance. There was a concerted effort to distinguish the "Southern way" from the North, and it was part of the push toward secession.

The groundswell in the Southern states had already been agitated by the powers that were more interested in industry than integrity. Slavery, while painful, heartbreaking, and monstrous, was not the core matter of the secession effort. It is a common fallacy, one of many, among historians who romanticize the roots of the Civil War, the evil of the South, and the empathy shown by Lincoln. In reality, it was about keeping the Union intact for Lincoln, and it was about leaving the Union for the South so that they could have control of the vast riches of the South that was built on the backs of slaves. Any excuse would do.

The Civil War purged the toxic buildup of those differences for the country and became the yardstick to measure the resolve of one man while blood was spilled in the mud along the battle lines.

The moment Lincoln won the election, which no one thought he would, the South capitalized on the deep-seated hatred they had for him. Some historians even go so far as to say that there was a wish on the part of the financiers in the background who wanted Lincoln to win so that they could use it as an excuse to secede. If they framed it in such a way that Lincoln would end slavery, then the South would mobilize against him and be up for splitting the country. Remember that the South had already made strong international ties and had become an advanced agricultural center. They did not need the North any longer.

Much of the wealth they gained came from exports to Europe, which included, but was not limited to, textiles and agriculture. They did not need the demand from the market created by their Northern neighbors. To be able to keep their margins and be cost-competitive, they needed their slaves, and they did not want anyone, including the federal government, continuously harping on the matter. They were under the impression that at some point it would become a problem, and they wanted to get out before it did.

As for Lincoln, there are a number of documents that give evidence to the fact that while slavery was a matter of concern because it tore at the fabric of morality, his main concern was to preserve the Union. In his letter to Horace Greeley, publisher of the *New York Tribune*, he made his deepest intentions clear that his priority was for the cohesion of the Union.

Lincoln was a long shot as a candidate who went on to win. Unlike today's typical presidential elections, it was not a two-way battle between one party and the other. There were numerous parties and factions at that time, and four of them had fielded a candidate in 1860. Lincoln represented the new Republican Party. Stephen Douglas, Lincoln's political nemesis, represented the Northern Democrats, John Bell represented the Constitutional Union Party, and John

Breckenridge represented the Southern Democrats.

If the battle was directly between Douglas and Lincoln, then the outcome would have been very different. Out of the four men, only Lincoln's policy stood out in stark contrast to the policies of the other three. Lincoln's position was so different from that in the South that he knew he would not be able to garner many votes there. His job was to appeal to the North.

On the election issues that mattered in the South, the other three men had similar positions and cannibalized each other at the ballot box. Their positions also alienated them in the North in favor of Lincoln.

The Democratic Party of the mid-nineteenth century was not the same as today's Democratic Party. In 1850, a major problem arose with respect to slavery that split the Democratic Party into two groups—the Northern Democratic Party and the Southern Democratic Party.

There were three aspects to slavery that you have to understand to have a better appreciation of the events of the time and to better understand Lincoln's point of view. The first school of thought was that slavery was unacceptable. The second was that slavery was necessary, and the third was that each person should have the right to decide on slavery within their own state. This was the foundation of the problem.

Then came the second layer to complicate matters. Lincoln didn't like slavery, but he merely wanted to hold the Missouri Compromise to its word and let the states that already had slavery on the books continue in the same way but disallow new territories to legalize slavery when they joined the Union.

This meant that the new territories that came after he was in office would not allow slavery. He was not looking to abolish slavery in the South; he was just trying to make sure that slavery didn't spread across to the new land and the states that came later. Lincoln was clear about this. He did not think that it would be fair to subject the industries of the South to a set of laws that put them at a disadvantage. He also believed that what had already been settled upon should not be reversed.

Those in the North were not interested in slavery and were morally aghast at the continued expansion of it and supported the idea of limiting slavery to some states that were already in the union. But those in the South wanted to expand it to the new territories as well. This was the contention. It was not about removing slavery in the South. It was about not allowing the new states to allow it.

The South was afraid of tipping the scales in Congress. If the new states were against slavery, then legislation that came up in Congress would be in favor of abolitionist ideology. The South read the tea leaves on this matter. As the West was unfolding, people there were not inclined to be slave states.

By the time of the election of 1860, the country was hotly debating the issue, and the South had already threatened once again to secede if slavery were on the table. The Democratic Party split to assuage its members on both sides of the debate, which proved to be a costly mistake.

The two sides of the party then fielded their own candidates for the general election—Breckenridge in the South and Douglas in the North. This, by itself, split the vote. If this had not happened, Lincoln would not have won the majority of the votes, and the Union would have taken a very different direction.

Every crisis is an opportunity, and to Lincoln the secession of the South, which happened on April 12, 1861, was the opportunity that allowed him to cease slavery across the board even in the states that were already in the Union during the Declaration of Independence.

Electoral math was not a major discipline in those days, and neither was scientific polling. The two halves of the Democratic Party were not sure what such a split would mean. It was the same way that Hitler rose to power in Germany—a split in the voting block delivers the power to the third party—a house divided. Ironically, the man who delivered his speech about "a house divided" became president himself because of a divided house. During his entire presidency, from before his inauguration to when he died, Lincoln presided over a divided house.

As we have now seen in the election of 2016, America is not straightforward when it comes to the presidential election. The Founding Fathers instituted something called the Electoral College, and that had the direct impact of tempering the power and vagrancy of the popular vote. The idea, as we learn from our civic textbooks, is to avoid the election of a popular president or something of a fad. That's a topic for another day. However, it was not just the 2016 election that resulted in an unexpected result. It also yielded an unexpected result in the 1860 presidential election.

The North had a larger share of the Electoral College and a larger share of the total population. It was more than double, with about twenty-three million in the North and nine million in the South. The South was divided in their choice, splitting the vote between its three candidates—

Bell, Breckenridge, and with a little left over for Douglas. Lincoln was pretty much shut out in the South. Each of the three candidates split the vote, which was small to begin with.

In the North, Breckenridge and Bell didn't gain any traction, and they were not looking to follow the policy that Douglas had laid out. They wanted the new territories to be free from slavery. That tipped the North in Lincoln's favor, but Douglas did manage to come close. If the vote in the South had not been split, it is almost a certainty that Douglas would have repeated his victory over Lincoln as he had done in the Senate race a few years earlier.

Nonetheless, Lincoln did win with the help of Republican grassroots in the North, with Hannibal Hamlin's faction of the pro-abolition fervor, and the word of print from Horace Greeley, among many others.

Chapter 2 - E Pluribus Unum

It certainly was a long road from Hodgenville, Kentucky, to Ford's Theatre. As perilous, tortuous, and bloody as it had been, it was the most righteous of journeys that was taken by any occupant of the president of the United States bar none. It was not a life that enhanced the status quo. It was a life that altered the course of American history.

As we advance over the course of the book, it is to be understood that Lincoln's life and history-altering influence was not limited to his life in the White House. It went far beyond that. What influenced him is altogether another matter and predates his own birth. It was molded by Puritanical views, lack of formal education, frontier antics, and backwoods mannerisms.

A look at the history of the man must also be mingled with the history of the environment and circumstances that surrounded him. At the broad view, the country we know today did not exist in form or culture as it did at the time Lincoln came into adulthood, and it certainly did not exist while he was at the height of his presidency or the Civil War.

For the first point, there were three Americas. The first America was not only geographically in the North but was also psychologically Northerners, or Yankees as Southerners referred to them. Being a Northerner was as much a state of mind as it was to be a Southerner.

Then there were those in the geographically southern areas of the country, which we think of as the South. Their mind-set was distinct and their lifestyles totally different from those in the North. As pilgrims arrived, the landscape changed rapidly, and as each year passed, not only was the country expanding westward, but each frontier town, each port city, and also towns expanded rapidly with new immigrants in search of a new life. Growth fueled evolution, and evolution created culture. Southern culture evolved until it was occupied by a certain aristocracy—what we think of as the Southern Lady and the Southern Gentlemen. It's not difficult to imagine.

Finally, there were those areas that were neither Northern states nor Southern states. These folks were part of the territory that was expanding westward but had not yet been included in the Union. Volumes have been written about these histories of the United States, but it would be too lengthy to list them here, so we shall look at them so that we have enough context to place the man who stood at the crossroads of all three mind-sets—the Northerner, the Southerner, and the frontiersman.

The Union was young at the time, with three forces tugging on it in different directions. There was the commercial force in terms of the resources that this new land possessed. From steel, oil, and gold in the ground to timber and agriculture above it, commerce was a major part of the American story and the primary force by the time Lincoln came to power. The world didn't stop just because the South seceded or because

Lincoln had become president. Commerce still proceeded, trade was still conducted, and fortunes were still being made—just think of Carnegie, Morgan, and Vanderbilt.

Then there were the alliances that created a delicate balance between the colonies and the Old World. It was, in part, driven by commerce, but it was also strategic in nature. The states that seceded from the Union were also the states that were the largest producers of cotton in the world, and Britain was a trading counterpart by far. Although Queen Victoria had initially proclaimed neutrality in the Civil War, as did all the other European countries, the British were gradually finding that it was better to be aligned with the South for commercial reasons.

This was also a major concern to Lincoln, who saw the dangers of the commercial ties the South had and the motivation to keep the status quo. The South definitely had the upper hand in negotiating the issue.

The merits of either side of the slavery debate are best left to another book for another time. For now, they are just there to place in context the resolve that Lincoln brought to the discussion and the steel he exemplified throughout the four years of his presidency.

There were two planks inherent in Lincoln's presidency: (1) his stated and vehement adherence to the constitution and (2) his love of the Union. The Civil War brought both to a head. Much of how he saw the Union was in part because of the role models that he adopted over the course of his readings.

Until Lincoln the United States of America was just a united federation of individual states. After Lincoln we became one nation, changing these united states to this United States. That was the true blessing of his presidency, and while he didn't see those actions and decisions in quite that romantic a light, the decisions he did make set the path to that conclusion, and for that we are eternally grateful because America is better when identified as one unit rather than an x number of parts. E Pluribus Unum was a motto that Lincoln adhered to and saw the wisdom of.

Chapter 3 - Phases of Life

"May the Almighty grant that the cause of truth, justice, and humanity, shall in no wise suffer at my hands."

Abraham Lincoln, May 21, 1860

For anyone who wants to truly appreciate the life of Abraham Lincoln, it can be best defined in four phases. His heritage and his youth are best placed in the first phase. It gives us the canvas on which to paint the accomplishments of the man against a backdrop of personal, societal, and systemic challenges.

The second covered his years as an adult that dovetailed into his time practicing law and his early political career. It was his time in law practice that raised his awareness of the nature of the country, what it meant, and the force to which it owed its existence. America is unique. It is not a country that was built the same way that others had been built. America was an experiment in self-governance.

His third phase was the period of time between his legislative career and the time he became president. It was during this time that he developed the manner of his thinking and the maturity of his planning. As the book will progressively reveal, Lincoln's ascendancy to the presidency and his reasons for doing so are not what they are always thought to be. It was not accidental. It was intentional. It was not altruistic. It was calculated. And, it was not enlightened. It was manipulative. In other words, he developed the skill necessary to be the consummate politician.

Then, finally, is the phase of his life that tested his mettle and changed the American promise from what it would have become to what it is today. This was the period that began the day he was elected and before he even took the oath of office. It was a combination of the issue of slavery, which was by all analytical accounts a convenient matter to discuss with the electorate but nonetheless a proxy of the real cause of battle. The South may have been at war because of slavery, but Lincoln was at war to hold the Union together. The issue of slavery, as important as it was back then, was second only to a subject that is largely misunderstood today and mostly forgotten.

By the time Lincoln had risen to prominence in Illinois, the South—those states that made up what was known to be the South—had already attempted to secede from the Union a number of times. The time just before the Civil War was by no means the first and only time.

As far back as the dawn of the age of Lincoln, Southern conservatism was a very different brand of thinking from what we think of conservatism to mean today.

Lincoln's studies had given him insight into the ideals of the men who were responsible for the founding of the country, and he began to see the wisdom of their perspective. Such men as Jefferson and Madison, who were initially opposed to certain common ideas, eventually started to see the benefit of one country comprised of numerous states. It was like a timber raft. The individual timbers would give it the stability it needed to carry more than just the same number of individual trunks would.

Lincoln, being a boat man, saw this clearly as well. Together, if they could work out their differences, they would be stronger against almost anything imaginable. Lincoln felt that the constant bickering of the states and the threats of secession had to stop. He also understood that such a goal could not be harnessed by just legislation. Something more needed to happen.

Lincoln was a well-read man. He had understood the playing field and how the dynamics had played out. In his writings, Lincoln had come to realize that the country was diverse because of three core factors. First was the geography and the climate. The American geography that he had personally experienced from his time in Kentucky and traveling up to Illinois allowed him to realize that the land was capable of different things in different places, causing people in those areas to ultimately behave differently. People are, after all, products of their environment.

For instance, it is not surprising that slavery flourished in the South because the plantations that were worked (before mechanization) were labor intensive and active almost throughout the year. In the North, different industries were prevalent and ones that did not necessarily lend themselves to intense slave labor.

The second reason the country was diverse in politics was that it was populated differently. The Southern states had low-density population centers, and most of the people were flung out and spread across a vast area. In was different in the North. The urban areas and countryside were more densely populated, which created a political landscape different from that of the South. In Congress, there were more representatives from the North than from the South. That meant that Southern interests, when they diverged from Northern interests, would be almost inconsequential in Congress. The North would automatically always have the power of the federal government behind them.

The South found this to be unacceptable and influenced their impression of the Northern states. It also resulted in the South choosing to deal directly in commerce outside the country. In time, they gradually did not see any advantages of remaining with the Union. It was not just in 1860 when the first seven states decided to leave the Union. Different combinations of Southern states had tried to do it in one form or another for the previous forty years since the Revolutionary War.

Lincoln had been studying the intricacies of the political landscape and the history of the United States. He was a student of history, law, and the actions of such men as Madison, Jefferson, and Washington. His candidacy, if he chose to run for president, would be a long shot. His aspirations to high office were motivated by a number of factors. He had been in Congress for years, and he had a solid grounding in the issues and understanding how the nuts and bolts of lawmaking and horse-trading were carried out.

He was trying to thread the political needle to be able to win the election. There were so many issues that he could run on, but every issue that he analyzed left him feeling that the issues that others saw to be what they championed were more popular in debate than his. The issues championed by his party were no longer sufficient to carry Lincoln to the destination of his dreams.

Lincoln was of the Whigs, the party founded by Henry Clay, one his childhood heroes. But within that party, Lincoln had done well as a four-term congressman and then descended into obscurity after retirement. He was nobody once he left congressional politics. To be able to aspire for higher office, he needed a grassroots movement that took interest in areas that were more widespread than just state issues, which were highly localized and did not offer any inspiration for a candidate with aspirations for national office.

When the Republican Party was founded some years later before the 1860 election, he realized that it could be his vehicle, if he chose, to ascend to the executive branch. In the first presidential election year since the forming of the Republican Party, Abraham Lincoln had been nominated as the vice-presidential candidate for the Republicans. The Republicans, however, lost the election that year at the presidential level but did surprisingly well at the congressional level. That year Democratic candidate James Buchanan was elected president.

Lincoln had no control over the manner in which the campaign was run. He was merely the VP candidate, and it was up to the man at the top of the ticket to determine the path and the crux of the campaign. It was also a new party at the time and was ultimately unproductive in its bid. The Republican Party was the second party that Lincoln had joined after being a Whig for the initial part of his political career.

The Whigs were popular between the 1830s and the 1850s, which was just before Lincoln had become active in congressional politics, and stayed relevant until he left. When he left Washington, D.C., he had every intention to return to the practice of law and do more for the country.

There are a number of reasons why Lincoln returned to the political stage after leaving Congress. Just as with all of us, our decisions are never based on just one reason. For Lincoln, too, there were many reasons, some consequential, some just a matter of convenience and preference. One of the reasons why he wanted to get back into the game was so that he could leave the house and put some distance between him and his wife. On the other end of the spectrum was a deeply personal reason—one that was rooted in his self-perception and self-esteem. Lincoln was a man who saw himself through the eyes of others. The years that he was away from the glare of the constituents he represented were some of the most difficult for him. He lived off the energy of public life, but he also hated the idea of losing. He had lost the race for the Senate to Stephen Douglas. There were two sides to his loss. The first was the low self-esteem that he suffered from. The second was his lack of a platform that would make sense. He needed to be able to reach across the landscape and sell himself. He knew that was not plausible.

The opportunity presented itself when the Kansas-Nebraska Bill passed Congress and was signed into law. The Kansas-Nebraska Act was a lightning rod that seemingly rolled back the Missouri Compromise and put slavery back in the center of the sphere of interest.

He knew that if he could meet every constituent, then he would not have a problem winning the contest. But there was no way to do that. He had to devise a different strategy, and he did.

Chapter 4 - Thomas Lincoln

One of the facets of any man is the childhood injections of morals, outlook, and motivations. Since children learn by mimicking, a boy, who soon sees the differences between his mother and his father, realizes that he should observe his father and be loved by his mother. When he observes his father, he finds a source to mimic and does the best he can to emulate. That is his psychological base. It is the way our species transmits continuity from one generation to the next while still maintaining the flexibility to adapt to changing conditions. From that paternal platform, his environment takes over, and he applies it, right or wrong, and faces the consequences, acceptable or otherwise, to gradually evolve and prompts a man to fill his own shoes.

Abraham Lincoln was the same. He was born into a family of love and hard work. His first glimpse of life came from seeing his father, while his first love was his mother. Much of Lincoln's character was set by the actions of his father and tempered by his mother's love. Getting to know his father then will go a long way in setting a sound foundation in understanding the sixteenth president.

Thomas Lincoln was the youngest son of Abraham Lincoln (the president's grandfather) and Bathsheba Lincoln. Mordecai and Josiah were older than Thomas and more successful later in life compared with young Thomas.

Thomas was the baby of the family both in terms of his age and that his two older brothers would take care of him. The family was well to do. They had been frontiersmen and built the homestead to be a profitable enterprise. Abraham Senior was a shrewd businessman and farmer, grounded in a strong work ethic, religion, and family. This was the fabric on which the Lincoln clan had been built on. When one is marinated in those qualities, it is hard to not become successful in life. This was born out by the president's two uncles, Mordecai and Josiah, who went on to become successful landowners and farmers.

For the first five years of his life, Thomas lived a fairly privileged childhood, being the center of everyone's attention. This had created a close bond with everyone in the family, but he primarily became close to his father.

By the time he was five years of age, little Thomas would wrap up his study and minimal chores and then follow his father in his daily work on the farm or when he had to go into town. He was by his father's side watching his brothers and just absorbing all it meant to be a Lincoln.

Part of their time together, Abraham Senior would relate the rich stories of the Lincoln family and how they came to Kentucky. Abraham's cousin, Daniel Boone the explorer, had made his way south from Virginia. They were among the first people to come to this part of the country. They went on to make connections and relationships with the Native Americans in the area.

Boone and Lincoln had done their best to expand the fur trade with local Indians in that part of the unexplored lands. Boone and Lincoln were enterprising young men who were looking to tap as much potential as they could on virgin soil. They traded for some time and became prosperous at it. It was said that Abraham Senior, who was a captain in the Revolutionary War and came from Amity, Pennsylvania, amassed more than $17,000 (equivalent to more than half a million dollars today) from this endeavor.

With part of that money, they set up a ranch and moved the whole family down to Kentucky. The business grew as the state did as well. The Lincoln family was well respected and well known across the district, then state of Kentucky.

When Thomas Lincoln (the president's father) was just eight years old, in May 1786, they were out in the field tending to the chores they typically did in the day. Mordecai was within shouting distance and closer to the barn, while Josiah was on another part of the property but also within earshot.

There was a contentious relationship between the settlers and the native tribes in the area, who would frequently lead raiding parties on the property of residents in the area. On a warm Kentucky summer day, they mounted an attack on the Lincoln farm. There hadn't been many attacks on the farm simply because Lincoln and Boone had always had a good relationship with the natives, and that made them stay clear of the Lincolns. But it was different that particular day.

As Thomas was crouching next to his father, the war party rode up the knoll and attacked both Lincolns. Abraham was struck and died instantly. The screaming commotion caught the attention of everyone within sight of the scene. Mordecai, the oldest of the Lincoln boys, had the presence of mind to run toward the barn, which was a short distance away, to retrieve a weapon.

In the meantime, the assassin had turned his sights on little Thomas, who was distraught. Fear aside, he was unable to process the killing of his father in such a bloody manner in front of him. He was too young and too scared to do anything.

Mordecai had also dispatched Josiah to the military stockade, Floyd's Station, located nearby on Beargrass Creek to get help. Mordecai was able to find his father's rifle and from a distance took aim at the man who was preparing to murder Thomas. From the barn, Mordecai killed him with one shot and saved his little brother.

At that moment, two things happened simultaneously. It changed the trajectory of Thomas, who became more withdrawn, while it emboldened Mordecai. The divergence of the two brothers forever altered their lives.

Not long thereafter Josiah arrived with the cavalry, and the war party rode away. This incident left a deep scar on young Thomas, who had the misfortune to have his father die in his arms and the fear of almost being killed himself.

That became the defining event in Thomas Lincoln's life, and subsequently the shadow of the father was cast on his son. Thomas could never seem to make the fortune that his brothers went on to make, and while Thomas was steadfast in his honesty and integrity, he never really could provide a comfortable life for his wife and children.

It was a key moment in the Lincoln family legacy. While the Lincolns that stemmed from Mordecai and Josiah did well, most of the others who descended from Thomas faded into the shadows of history. The other Lincolns had worked hard and provided for their family, and the typical American dream unfolded in front of them. Thomas, on the other hand, was the exact opposite.

After that incident, Thomas retreated into a shell, which was to be expected considering what he had just witnessed. His family gave him some time to recover, but even after two years he was still less engaged in life than everyone else in the household.

His academics suffered and so did his time with chores. He did, however, enjoy being alone and working with wood. He had some understanding of agriculture and farming but not to the degree any of his siblings did, and so he seemed to not be as successful as his father and brothers. Thomas was also prone to melancholy and fear. He was not able to muster any sort of risk tolerance or put aside any of his fear of doing almost anything that normal people would. Even his moods were not stable. The grew more despondent as he grew older and began spending hours in silence or talking about the old days when he would help his father and the time his father was murdered.

He drifted from one property to the next, earning a meager living with his woodworking skills. He had poor business acumen and little farming instinct. He even purchased land to farm that was filled with rocks and boulders, and he was unable to make anything of it. This inability to make a life like the one his brothers had frustrated him to a high degree. But whatever share of intelligence that had been taken away from him on that summer morning in Kentucky, it hadn't touched a sliver of his honesty, which he was liberally endowed with.

The one thing that determined his actions and fueled his thoughts was the nature of honesty that he eventually passed down to his son, who became president. He did not live long enough to see his son try for the vice presidency or eventually be elected president.

Within a decade of Thomas losing his father, he had moved to neighboring Washington County and away from the rest of his family. He continued with his carpentry work to provide for himself. His desire to move away from his family was not unlike what would eventually be the same trajectory that his son, Abraham, would do many years later.

He was not the kind of person who would settle down for long in one place. After spending a few years in Washington County, Thomas decided that he would find his calling by purchasing a farm, which he did with some of his inheritance and money that he had saved.

The 238-acre farm was located in Kentucky's Hardin County, just about fifty miles south-southwest of Louisville, Kentucky. He moved there in 1802 and started to work the farm and make a living. It was a time that he seemed to be coming out of his darkness. He was about 5' 10" tall, much shorter than his son would be later in life, and he weighed 190 lbs. Thomas was not the quickest on his feet, choosing to do work that didn't require a lot of movement.

The one strong feature that seemed to be a major part of his character was his frugality. When one is frugal, there are numerous benefits that arise, not least of which is the ability to save money. Frugality also allows the person to not be swayed and predisposed to lavish distractions. Thomas was certainly that way. He was not a person who was lavish or predisposed to a lifestyle of his standard, much less one that was above it. That kept him out of trouble. Lincoln, the president, observed this while he was growing up. There was not one pretentious bone in his body just as there were none in his father's.

In 1806, four years after settling in Washington County, and reducing his time on the farm in exchange for working as a carpenter in Elizabethtown, Thomas met a young seamstress who used to work in the Washington-Hardin area. Her job would take her from one county to the next, spending time in the homes where she worked. Nancy Hanks and Thomas Lincoln courted that same year and then married on June 12. After the wedding, they moved into a cabin close to where he worked with plans to start a family. As a family, they joined the congregation of the Little Mount Separate Baptist Church.

This church was in contention and had split from the South Fork Baptist Church in Hardin over the issue of slavery in 1807. The Lincolns were resolutely antislavery even back then, as they felt that it was not consistent with Bible teaching. Their first child, Sarah, was born in 1807.

After a short time in Elizabethtown, they moved to another cabin in Sinking Spring Farm in Nolan Creek just a few miles from the church and just outside Hodgenville. Here on a cold Sunday morning before daybreak, after a long night in labor, Nancy Lincoln, with the help of a young midwife, gave birth to a baby boy they named after his grandfather. It was April 12, 1809.

The delivery had weakened Nancy to the point that she lost a lot of weight after the birth. The couple tried for a third child not long after that and was blessed for a short while with another little boy. They named him Thomas, but he died shortly afterward much to the deep sorrow of his mother. The darkness rushed back into Thomas' life at that point, and the time for dark clouds and gloom returned after a long absence.

Chapter 5 - Development

Abraham Lincoln, son to Thomas Lincoln and grandson to his namesake, was born in the barest of log cabins in the backwoods of Hodgenville, Kentucky. Today, the town is populated with just over a thousand people, a stark contrast to the days when the Lincolns first arrived in the area. Back then it didn't even have so much as a High Street, and one's closest neighbor would have been a half a day's walk away.

Forget for a moment the weight of Lincoln's actions and how history has placed him on the pedestal that few occupy, and look at him as just any man. That would be the best way to start simply because before the choices and trials came to pass, he was nothing more and nothing less. At a young age, young Lincoln was of a happy disposition and good manners.

Lincoln had just about twelve months of schooling, cumulatively, across his entire life. He never saw the inside of a classroom at a young age as children do today, and when he did, he was already much older and only did so infrequently. This upbringing and lack of any significant schooling resulted in a naturally unpolished demeanor, although that was not the measure of his kindness. His rough edges were more so in contrast with the refined ways of the upper class but not subpar to it. He may not have known how to say something harsh in gentle terms, but he knew how to be gentle in harsh terms. It was his mark of sincerity and sensitivity.

Unlike men of success in that period of time, Lincoln had not entered the fray with a strong educational background and one that was polished in a way that Dickens referred to as gentlemen of sorts. In fact, Lincoln's mannerisms were gruff, even if they were on the right side of righteousness. It would be easy to mistake Lincoln for a loser if you were to see him in his element as a youth. Between the lack of formal education, his backwoods mannerisms, and his unusual appearance in stature and countenance, not many people would peg him for someone who had a resolve of steel and the ability to teach himself what he didn't know.

After teaching himself how to read, he realized there were two kinds of language that were spoken. The first was the kind that he and his fellow backwoodsmen engaged in, and the other was the language that the educated spoke.

Lincoln quickly realized that his peaceful demeanor and Puritan values were better represented by the version of communication that one would classify as being educated. The problem was that this occurred around the time when he was nearly in his late teens, and going to school was no longer a viable option. He also didn't have the opportunity to come into contact with men of eloquent demeanor and a polished veneer.

What he lacked in eloquence, however, he made up for in heart and intelligence. By heart, of course, we mean that he had the tenacity and stamina to do what needed to be done. Don't confuse heart with the romanticism of pity, empathy, or sympathy. Once he realized that what he had to do was improve the way he spoke, he looked around for books that would give him a better grasp of the language. What he found was a book on grammar. He found that *A New Guide to the English Tongue* by Thomas Dilworth was something that would be of great help, and he set about to get a copy.

The closest one that he could borrow was a few miles outside town, and so he walked to ask its owner if he could borrow the book. He was successful and studied it repeatedly from cover to cover and altered the way he spoke and the eloquence in the way he wrote. It allowed him to bridge the gap between the fate of his fortunes to pulling himself up by the scruff of his collar to a point that he could eloquently participate later in life in the Lincoln-Douglas debates, which set the trajectory for him to be elected president.

By the time Lincoln was seven years old, his family had moved to Indiana. It was 1816, and James Madison was president of the United States. His sister, Sarah, was nine, and life was hard enough in frontier lands and frontier times, but it was more so for the Lincolns. Southern Indiana was the new frontier during that time, and its population was still scarce, but opportunities abounded, which is what Thomas Lincoln was looking for.

They staked their claim on a 160-acre plot and quickly set about to build a cabin as winter approached. Thomas was an able carpenter, and he often had little Abraham in tow, helping him with the chores. In time, Thomas made a name for himself in the vicinity and began taking on carpentry work to keep up the family and the homestead. Thomas was a good carpenter. His honesty and integrity compelled him to produce work that was meticulous and well-crafted. Abraham watched and learned and soon was able to everything with wood, from picking the tree that needed to be felled to designing the furniture and assembling the final product.

Even without trade school and formal education, wood and carpentry became second nature to Abraham. Woodworking was one of the two loves of his life. Just like his father. His second was reading. Even though he did not have much formal education, he taught himself to read and became a voracious reader. The following is a list of the consequential books he read in his lifetime.

Autobiography of Benjamin Franklin by Benjamin Franklin

Ancient History by Charles Rollins

Robinson Crusoe by Daniel Defoe

Complete Works of Edgar Allen Poe

Decline and Fall of the Roman Empire by Edward Gibbon

Geometry by Euclid

Fanny, With Other Poems by Fitz-Greene Halleck

Sociology for the South by George Fitzhugh

Poems by Henry Longfellow

Commentaries on American Law by James Kent

An Authentic Narrative of the Loss of the American Brig Commerce by James Riley

Joe Miller's Book of Jests by Joe Miller

Mormonism by John Hyde

Liberty by John Stuart Mill

Journals and Debates of the Federal Constitution by Jonathan Elliot

Analogy of Religion by Joseph Butler

The Life of George Washington by Mason L. Weems

Poems by Oliver Wendell Holmes

Lives of Emperors by Plutarch

The Theory and Practice of Surveying by Robert Gibson

History of Illinois by Thomas Ford

Poems by Thomas Hood

Poems by William Knox

Lessons in Elocution by William Scott

Complete Works of William Shakespeare

There are two things of note from this list. First, this is not the full extent of his reading list. There were other books that he surely must have read. These are just the books that he kept safely and treasured them. They followed him from Illinois to Washington, D.C., and were later passed to his son Robert Todd Lincoln.

Second, it is also said by a number of different sources that Lincoln had memorized almost all the poems that he was exposed to in the books that are on this list. Poetry was the tonic that seemed to sooth his vexed mind when the days grew dark in his mind.

There is plenty of evidence that even though he didn't attend school because it was either too far away or there was no reliable transportation to get him that far, his parents did give him the encouragement that prompted him to read. He did more however.

There are numerous anecdotes about his endeavors to find books. The early to mid-eighteenth century was a period not known for its easy availability of books. It was hard to find one and one of the reasons why Andrew Carnegie started building more than two thousand libraries across the United States starting in 1883. But at this point while Lincoln was still a young adolescent in Kentucky and then in Indiana, few libraries were available.

He typically did not know if a book on a particular subject existed. He would just be interested in a subject and then would ask a teacher in town or someone he knew was educated, and they would suggest a title or two. He'd then go on a sort of treasure hunt to look for that book until he found it. Once he got the book, he would write down quotes or entire sections from it in his own notebook or on paper. He would then return the book. Lincoln made a list of all the books that stuck him, and when he had the opportunity, he would purchase a copy. He had a sense of desire to be able to find more knowledge by sheer curiosity and self-awareness. It was a display of total awareness because it is hardly common to find a person who knows what they do not know and finds the information to fill that void.

Lincoln also had the habit of visiting the drugstore or the general store wherever he visited. Whenever he traveled, even when he sailed down the Mississippi River to New

Orleans, he stopped at places that sold books and looked for what he could afford. What he couldn't afford, he waited until an opportunity presented itself.

During the time he would chop wood for work, he would spend his free time reading his law books or the state's constitution, and when he worked at the grocery store, he would spend the quiet hours lying on the counter and reading whatever book he had just borrowed, bought, or something he had already read. Whenever the store owner would stock books (which rarely happened), he would carefully read those, too, and make sure he did not crease them for anyone who eventually bought them.

When Lincoln got to the White House, the South had already seceded, and when the war eventually erupted, he would find solace in the list of books that he thought were his best sources of comfort. He still made time to read even in the midst of heavy workloads, meetings, strategy considerations, and spending time with his family. Reading was his form of meditation.

Books aside, Lincoln was given to reading as a natural extension of his intellect. He read every bill that came to his desk for his signature. He read every report and every analysis. In the midst of all this, he was also a hopeless romantic. Putting aside his chiseled features and his lanky stature, he was soft on the inside and just wanted to hear the kind words that he took the trouble to utter to others. Words moved and soothed him. It wasn't after a long marriage that Mary Lincoln had come to understand this side of him. For a large portion of their marriage, her vocabulary, her tenor, and her tone were not of the same flavor as Lincoln, which was deeply saddening for him, but he never said a word about it.

Chapter 6 - Young Adulthood

In 1816, the Lincolns moved to a small community in Perry County. It was on the banks of Little Pigeon Creek in southern Indiana. This was virgin country and another piece of land that the Lincolns had come to that was frontier land. They seemed to always be on the leading edge of American expansion, just as little Thomas had remembered his father doing when he was five years old. Thomas Lincoln seems to have been in a psychological loop that kept him always trying but never really succeeding.

Lincoln was now seven years old and having a great time exploring the country. He enjoyed the family's move from Kentucky to Indiana. They left Kentucky in the beginning of summer and used the warm weather and easier conditions through the forest and mountain trails. It took them the whole summer to make the journey.

Lincoln would later remember this trip as one of his most pleasant. It was filled with adventure, his parents were with him, he spent time talking to his father, and as the case with many children, he just loved being on the road. It was the thrill of the unknown since this was the first time he had been outside Kentucky.

In the nineteenth century, out on the frontier, being a seven-year-old was almost like being a man. When Lincoln and his family reached Indiana, it felt almost like a world away in some aspects but felt no different in other aspects. The work, however, was tougher than usual. The land they settled on was densely forested and required clearing, which Thomas and Abraham did by themselves at first.

The family was accustomed to frugality, and the tight situations they faced in the wake of the move to Indiana was not something that was too stressful for the them. They had their muskets and all the wood they needed. So, hunting and cooking what they hunted kept them fed. What they needed to do was clear the land and use the lumber to build a cabin. Until that was done, they spent the nights in tents while the weather was still not too cold. By the time winter came, they hadn't finished the house, and much of it was still laid bare for the elements. But Abraham was still happy with all that was happening. He was starting to feel like a man, and the world was his playground.

Their first winter passed with the settling in process. It was colder than what they had been used to, and the chores were a welcome activity because it kept them active and warmer. Abraham fell asleep every night before his head could hit the pillow, totally exhausted from the chores of the day.

The entire family would be up at dawn. On most mornings and the nights that followed, they would be without light. Candles were a luxury, but the roaring fire that Thomas would build to combat the cold that entered the house was enough to give them the light they needed.

That first winter seemed to last forever. When spring finally arrived and the land began to thaw, the Lincolns got back to work and began putting a barrier to their home so that they could be sheltered from the elements. Abraham had much to learn, and he watched intently and did exactly what he needed to do to learn every ounce of skill from his father.

The days rolled into seasons very rapidly and especially so for a family having to pull together out on the leading edge of a westward-pushing frontier with no services to rely on. Out in the wilderness, there were no stores one could rely on and no drugstore to provide relief. Each man and his family had to rely on their resourcefulness to be able to live.

Getting sick in the outdoors is also a dicey affair. Simple ailments can be dealt with by placebos telling the mind to make itself well, or some concoctions can indeed have an effect, but some problems need expert help. Nancy Hanks Lincoln, Abraham's mother, was in need of such help.

She died from an illness related to the milk she had consumed. It was something that was common at the time in frontier towns, where services were initially scarce, and each family fended for themselves. The milk sickness, as it was referred to, was fairly common and involved contaminated milk of a cow that had grazed on snakeroot.

Mrs. Lincoln had kindly gone to attend to a neighbor's sick family, where she contracted it herself and died shortly thereafter. Her death was, among the rest of the family, the hardest on nine-year-old Abraham, who was close to his mother.

His mother had been his academic inspiration, as it was she who had introduced him to the benefits of learning, even though she and her husband were not able to read and write. With her passing, it became a silent household, as Thomas Lincoln found it too hard to manage a family alone and not have the counsel and aid of a woman in the home. At the time, he became president, Lincoln wrote that he owed all that he had become to the guidance and love of his mother.

Being carpenters, the two Lincoln men felled the necessary timber from their land and whipsawed the planks needed for the coffin and laid Nancy Lincoln in the ground under the shade of the thick forest that surrounded the Lincoln homestead. Lincoln did not stop crying the whole time.

The absence of a softer touch in the Lincoln home, especially someone to guide young Abraham and be an example to the elder Sarah, prompted Thomas Lincoln to return to Kentucky in 1819 with the sole intention to find a wife to take back to Indiana. When he returned, he found Sarah Johnston, the lady that he had once wooed but was unsuccessful in courting before he had met Nancy Hanks. But this time fate dealt him a different result with Sarah Bush Johnston, as the man she had married had also passed, and she was a widow with two children of her own. This time she was more amenable to his advances, and they were married, and she returned with him to Indiana.

Not only was she a courageous woman, but she was also kind and loving, and she easily integrated the household, taking Sarah and Abraham under her wing and guiding them as her own.

The home routine with a stepmother and the carpentry that he performed with his father and the avalanche of reading that he could fit into his busy schedule maintained a stable life for Lincoln at this point. By the time he was nineteen in 1828, he was already six feet four inches in height and slender from the hard life he lived as an active frontiersman.

John Quincy Adams was president at this point when another catastrophe struck the Lincoln family. Abraham's sister, Sarah, passed away during childbirth at the age of twenty-one. This second loss was devastating to him but combined with the loss of his mother ten years earlier and the eventual loss of his son while he was president were the three personal losses that steeled his character and brought focus to his mind. A lesser man would have allowed the loss to dictate his actions, but Abraham Lincoln was not an ordinary backwoods frontier man. He was someone who had greater aspirations for his contribution and higher ideas for all mankind.

Chapter 7 - Spreading His Wings

Wanting to spread his wings and increase the household income, Lincoln found work in town, and it happened to be with the richest man in the area—James Gentry. The task was simple. Lincoln was to accompany Gentry's son on a flatboat barge carrying supplies down the Mississippi River to New Orleans. The adventure was one that appealed to him, and the river, the boat, and the trip left a deep impression on his young and adventurous mind.

There was one other event on that trip that disturbed him enough to leave a lasting impression. When they reached New Orleans, while still on the flatboat, Lincoln observed for the first but not the last time the auction of slaves. The entire scene and the indignity of the buying and selling of humans disturbed him deeply and left a scar that never left him. The emancipation of slaves has been accredited to Lincoln, and it was a major part of his life, but liberating millions of people from the shackles of abuse does not assuage the horrors that preceded it.

On that trip, he discovered that he was a natural when it came to navigating the river and handling the barge. He was naturally made whole again by the open air that immersed him. He conducted his responsibilities exquisitely and went beyond the expectations of the man who hired him. It was always a characteristic of Lincoln to give more than was expected.

When he returned to Indiana, he continued to work odd jobs for Gentry's store, which also happened to be the place locals would gather and discuss the hottest topics in politics at the time. This is the first documented instance of Lincoln's interest in politics, and it suited him well. His interest in reading and the desire to increase his oratory powers paid off, as he was able to articulate his points better than the typical customer at the store.

This slide into politics was purely by accident, and he started to get a view of policies and positions from a grassroots perspective. It was an opportunity that he didn't appreciate at that time to be critical to his future successes. The more he listened to the different perspectives, the more it brought about his own views and polished his own thoughts on the matter. The more he thought about different issues, the more he began to take positions on matters of the day, but he was still far from diving into politics.

Back home, Thomas Lincoln had begun to do well in his business. Father and son had seemingly left their darker days behind and embraced the virtues of industry by putting their mind and backs to good use.

With Thomas Lincoln doing well in his business and Abraham Lincoln doing well with his repertoire of odd jobs, the Lincolns' stay in Indiana seemed to take on an air of prosperity. Between his odd jobs, his continued reading, his expanding social circle, and his love of the river, he was at the pinnacle of his youth.

As time passed, the river was more enticing to the younger Lincoln, and he started to work on other river-based opportunities. He eventually yielded to his enterprising spirit and built his own scow that would ferry passengers from the shore to riverboats sailing on the river.

By the time Lincoln was twenty-one, it was 1830, Adams was still president, and there was a threat of another breakout of the milk disease. Lincoln Senior did not cozy up to those prospects and decided to move to Illinois, a non-slaveholding state.

The Lincoln family moved to Illinois in March 1830 and settled by the Sangamon River, just south of today's Decatur. The family built a log cabin and fenced off close to ten acres of land, which they then farmed. With the earlier experience of navigating down the Mississippi River, the younger Lincoln set about finding a job in the area that would use his boating and navigation ability.

Soon after he turned twenty-two, Lincoln moved to New Salem. His time in New Salem was occupied initially with odd jobs to survive when he came upon Denton Offutt. He assisted Offutt with building a cargo barge when they couldn't find one to take Offutt's supplies down to New Orleans by the river network. The Sangamon River that Lincoln was intimately familiar with led to the Illinois River and then to the Mississippi River, which gave them direct passage to New Orleans.

Lincoln and three others offered to build a flatboat, which Offutt agreed to and paid each man $12 a month. Lincoln built the flatboat, which was eighty feet long. It proved sufficient to handle all the goods that Offutt was planning to have shipped down to New Orleans and to bring other goods back on the return trip.

The problem was that the barge ran aground in the Sangamon River. Lincoln put his back into it and with considerable effort and toil eventually freed the boat laden with bacon and supplies headed south. Lincoln's design for the flatboat was eventually patented, and until today day Lincoln is the only president in history to hold a patent under his name.

Offutt liked what he saw in Lincoln and offered him a job as his assistant in a new store that he was planning to open. It was hard to find a person who was as honest as he was, with that much integrity, and who was also willing to work for a fair wage. New Salem was a new frontier village at the time, hardly even three years old, with a population of less than a hundred people. It has since vanished from the map, and all that stands in its place is Lincoln's New Salem built in memory of the president.

As one with any notion of frontier living could comprehend, the town was filled with travelers who were headed west across the northern route. It wasn't one of the major trails westward, but it was sufficiently busy to warrant the expansion of a frontier post, and that expansion happened rapidly, as did the expansion in other areas of Illinois. The primary pastime among the men here was a toss-up between drinking whiskey and cockfighting. Lincoln, however, managed to remain strict in his abstinence from spirits save one or two occasions at most.

One such occasion that is a popular anecdote told about Lincoln in his youth was the incident where he lifted overhead a barrel of whiskey and proceeded to drink directly from it. The story was more a testament to his unassuming strength given his tall but slender stature. Otherwise, Lincoln was a teetotaler.

Between the time of the offer and the store actually opened, it took some time and so, once again, Lincoln took on odd jobs. Here he met Mentor Graham, a schoolmaster and went to work for him as a clerk. As the clerk, he came into contact with other residents of the area and became popular among them. He also worked as a rail splitter and took on various boating jobs on the Sangamon.

It took Offutt about a year to finally get the store set up, and Lincoln went on to work at the store, and this opened up his fortunes by increasing the number of people he came into contact with. The time at Offutt's store gave him two important opportunities: (1) it allowed him to come into contact with the community at large, and (2) it allowed him the time to read and brush up on language and politics.

It was here at the store on the counter that Lincoln would lie on his back and read. It wasn't just grammar that he worked on; in his free time, he also worked on his arithmetic and read Euclid's treatise on geometry. It is not a book that has the reputation of being easy reading. Yet, it was Lincoln's interest to understand this branch of mathematics from the man who was instrumental in its development.

The time he had spent meeting all those people contributed to his popularity, which he gained from his eloquent disposition. That, in addition to his infamous fistfights that happened to protect the store against bullies and thugs who were terrorizing the town's businesspeople, imbued on him an air of righteousness. On top of all this, his experience with the Sangamon River and boatmanship down the Mississippi River gave him numerous ideas of how the town could benefit from increasing the navigability of the Sangamon River. All these individual and seemingly disjointed matters directed him to become a candidate in the election for state legislator.

This was not to be, however, as his campaign to run for office was interrupted when he joined the 31st Regiment of the Illinois militia that year when there was an Indian uprising. The Indian chief Black Hawk had tried to resettle east of the Mississippi River, but the attempt was misconstrued by the settlers, and the volatile situation soon led to the entry of other tribes, and a full-blown armed conflict ensued.

In Illinois, Lincoln's company had elected him captain, and in the four months of the Black Hawk War, Lincoln experienced the life of the militia but without seeing any battles. It so happened that one Jefferson Davis was also in the war at the same time as Lincoln. He would go on to become the first, and last, president of the Confederacy. Lincoln's most notable incident during the war was when his company caught a member of the tribe and were about to hang him when Lincoln stepped in to stop the hanging.

When the war ended, Lincoln returned and threw his hat once more into the election for the state legislature. He announced his candidacy with this short speech:

"Fellow Citizens, I presume you all know who I am. I am humble Abraham Lincoln. I have been solicited by many friends to become a candidate for the Legislature. My politics are short and sweet like the old woman's dance. I am in favor of a national bank. I am in favor of the internal improvement system and a high protective tariff. These are my sentiments and political principles. If elected, I shall be thankful; if not, it will be all the same."

This was, essentially, his policy position statement. His position also included the advocacy of laws that stopped usury and laws that improved education. It happened that these principles reflected those of the Whig Party.

The Whig Party was one of the four major parties during the nineteenth century in the United States. Its founder, Henry Clay, was one of Lincoln's role models, and we can take two things from this fact. Clay's view of America was one that either appealed to Lincoln's puritanical values or was one that molded his values. In either case, his education and usury planks of policy were taken directly from Henry Clay.

The problem was that the Whig Party didn't have much footing in Illinois at the time, which was mostly supported the Democratic Party and the presidency of Andrew Johnson. The point to note is that while it is not certain how he came to adopt Clay's points of view and the foundation of the Whig Party, it was in direct opposition to the people who were predominantly around him in southern Illinois and Illinois as a whole. As such, his candidacy for the state legislature in 1832 failed.

What's interesting, though, is that while his views were totally different from most people's, he did manage to get most of the votes of his immediate neighborhood, suggesting that his likability among the people who knew him dominated the outcome more than his policy, which they opposed.

With the election loss and without any money in his pocket, Lincoln was attracted to the study of law. When he was younger, he had read books on state law, but he realized that law was central to the country, the states, and the harmony and prosperity of the people. His desire to read law increased over time, and he would devour books on the subject whenever he could. However, his priority at the time was to find work and support himself, and among the things he considered becoming the town's blacksmith, but that didn't happen. Instead, he used his good credit and honesty to purchase half a share of a store in New Salem. The other share was sold to a Mr. Berry for credit as well.

This, however, didn't go well in any way. It actually ended very poorly for Lincoln, who ended up taking fifteen years to pay down the debt that he incurred. The idea of a general store in New Salem was not new, and there were other stores, including the one Offutt opened that eventually went out of business. In this case, the partners who sold the store to Lincoln and Berry were also not doing well and saw the proverbial writing on the wall. That was the reason why they were willing to let it go on credit. Two things sealed the fate of the endeavor. The first was that Berry drank the liquor that was in inventory, and the store was not selling as much as it needed to keep things going. In the end, Lincoln and Berry sold the failing store in 1833 to two other entrepreneurs, but they couldn't handle the burden of a failing store and instead disappeared. That left Berry and Lincoln fully liable for the outstanding sums to the original owners. Before long, Berry died from alcohol abuse, which put the full value of the outstanding debt on Lincoln's shoulders.

That was the last time he invested his time and reputation on a business. Finally, after saving and working at various jobs and becoming prosperous, it took him fifteen years to fully pay the original sum that was agreed to. He could have sought bankruptcy protection from the courts, but he felt that would be dishonorable and decided to pay it all off over time.

His desire to pay off his debt even though it could have been pared down or totally abolished was something that earned Lincoln the epithet of Honest Abe. It was almost a character flaw the level to which he would take his honesty, and it was the same trait that probably made him stand on the side he did when it came time to fight the Civil War. His loyalty to the Constitution the way he saw it made all the difference in the world. While life was certainly important and the blood that spilled in the mud across the country was fully in his mind, his ideals, loyalty to the Union, and adherence to the Constitution made him who he was.

His penny-pinching days in the wake of the New Salem store affair stuck with him, and it seemed that for all the poverty that he had faced growing up he was never one to desire wealth. He felt that wealth was a distraction and something he didn't need. The only thing that he spent money on and even then in a limited fashion was his hats.

Poverty affects people in different ways when growing up. In some cases, poverty brings about a deep desire to become wealthy so that the pain of poverty can seemingly be avoided and remedied. Then there is the consequence of poverty, where one gains strength from knowing that poverty is not extinguished by being wealthy but by not desiring unnecessary, or in the words of Lincoln, "superfluous needs."

Whatever the problem, Lincoln's desire to advance in the world of politics was beginning to gain traction, and his eloquence began to match his ambition. His ideals were starkly different from the locality where he came from, and the typical voter was not fully educated in the nuances of legislation or its ramifications. One of those ramifications came about in terms of the financial impact that different actions brought and was something Lincoln was not totally suited for. Unfortunately, that was exactly what the Illinois legislature was grappling with—economic issues. The Whigs and the Democrats had a battle on their hands concerning economics, and as much as Lincoln tried to jump in, he just did not have the economic sense to contribute positively. Economics, finance, and accounting just didn't come naturally to him. Even his greatest admirers and fans considered him weak in this area, and so did he.

Politics didn't pay the bills, and so he needed to find a way to support himself, and it was by happenstance and word of mouth that he was offered a position to be the assistant surveyor by John Calhoun (not to be confused with John C. Calhoun, former U.S. vice president).

Calhoun was the county surveyor and a lawyer by profession. He was also a staunch Democrat as were many others in southern Illinois. The two men debated furiously over politics, but they also had a high regard for one another. Back then it was easy to have a difference of opinion among gentlemen and yet retain the necessary respect. Upon securing the job, he then sought the assistance of Mentor Graham, who pointed him in the right direction to find information and learn about surveying. Most of his surveys that can be found were ones that are evidence to Lincoln's accurate nature and high standards of work.

He advanced from being a surveyor to becoming postmaster of New Salem, and by the time 1834 rolled around, he decided to run for office again. This time instead of giving speeches to a sea of listeners, he decided to capitalize on his strength, which was to meet and chat with as many constituents in his district as possible. The plan worked, as they liked him more than they disliked the Whig Party.

In his second attempt for a seat in the Illinois State Legislature, Lincoln was able to pull off an upset win. On August 4, 1834, when Lincoln was twenty-five years old, Andrew Jackson was president, and the Illinois state capital was located in Vandalia, Abraham Lincoln won his seat with 1,376 votes.

Upon winning, Lincoln felt the need to prepare for the job, and since the job of being a legislator was all about knowing the law, and, more importantly, crafting the law, he used his time before heading up to Vandalia to study the means to craft law and to understand the law itself. He borrowed what he needed from John Todd

Stuart, a fellow Kentuckian and lawyer, and he purchased what he could from auctions.

The first session of the legislature began on December 1, 1834, and ended on February 13, 1835. Between the time he was elected and the time he left for Vandalia, Lincoln managed to become familiar with the language of legislation and understand the platform of the Whig Party that he championed. He took his time, but he was able to get a good grasp of drafting legislation, and he mastered the technicalities that are peculiar to drafting bills. When the session ended and he returned to New Salem, he had made $158.

When he got back to New Salem, he returned to his job as postmaster and continued his surveying responsibilities while he pursued his endeavor to become a lawyer. Reading occupied most of his time, where he made the effort to master complex documents and memorizing relevant passages.

Chapter 8 - First True Love

"Character is like a tree and reputation like its shadow. The shadow is what we think of it; the tree is the real thing."

Abraham Lincoln

Much of Lincoln's adult life was characterized by loneliness. Between his "nerdy" qualities, his silence, and his awkward physical features, it was not easy for him to be sociable. As much as he was easily liked among members of his same gender, he was rather alienated by members of the opposite sex. You could think of Lincoln as the tortoise in the tale of the tortoise and the hare. He was slow but sure, and he was the same way in relationships as well.

Not to be mistaken, Lincoln was not a shy person in general or afraid of the opposite sex. He just preferred to not be engaged in conversation with them whenever possible. If confronted by a lady, he was always polite, chivalrous, and courteous. Deep inside, however, he had insecurities about his appearance, which was a direct result of his impoverished youth. He and J.P. Morgan, a man born almost three decades after him, shared the same path inters of self-conscious debilitation and ambition all wrapped up in one. Both were silent men, and both were highly driven. The point here being that he was highly self-critical of his appearance.

However, as we all know that no matter how shy one is or how gregarious we can be, there comes a time that even the most cloistered of hearts will fall in love. As did Lincoln. His first love, and only true love, was one Miss Ann Rutledge.

Ms. Rutledge happened to be the daughter of a store and inn. She, too, hailed from Kentucky, which provided Lincoln with some semblance of familiarity and some memory of maternal origin. It was common to find Kentuckians across the border in Indiana, especially those who wanted to return to a more civilized life.

Lincoln arrived in New Salem, Kentucky, in 1831. He was an awkward twenty-two-year-old who was looking to make a living on his own. He didn't have a home in New Salem and chose to live at an inn—the same inn owned by Mr. Rutledge, Ann's father.

Lincoln first saw Ann a few days after arriving at the inn and was instantly attracted to her. He was clearly smitten by her looks and swept away by her demeanor.

He described her eloquently as someone of exquisite beauty, charm, and grace—all qualities that Lincoln seemed to cherish. She was, according to him, the prettiest of God's creatures that he had ever seen or would ever see in the future. She was blessed with uncharacteristic auburn hair and deep blue eyes, standing about 5'2". Her slender silhouette and fair complexion were atypical of the frontier community that Lincoln was used to.

She was known and loved by all in the area, with a bevy of suitors hoping to intersect the rest of their lives with hers. Lincoln was extremely attracted to her and hoped to marry her. According to William Herndon, Lincoln's law partner, he had found some documentary evidence that spoke of Lincoln's heartbreak and that Ms. Rutledge was the love of his life. It was not something that former First Lady Mary Todd Lincoln was too pleased to hear. Considering Lincoln's meticulous journaling and Mr. Herndon's integrity, there is not much doubt that one could ascribe to the possibility that Lincoln did feel strikingly for Ms. Rutledge, who died of an illness. It was recorded that after her passing Lincoln was standing near her grave and commented to a close associate, "My heart lies buried there."

When they first saw each other, he was prevented from making much headway for a number of reasons. He didn't believe that he was ready to make a commitment, but that was not the real problem, which was that he had low self-esteem and saw himself unworthy of someone so exquisite.

To complicate matters, it came to be known that she was in love with someone. She eventually got engaged to him, and all seemed lost to Lincoln. It seemed as though he had missed his chance, and this fed into his already diminished self-esteem. He was heartbroken.

She was engaged to one John McNamara, who was from the East Coast. He struck Lincoln as a suspicious character, but he said nothing of it since it could be misconstrued, and it was not proper to impugn another man's character on less than solid evidence.

McNamara made close friendships and developed a life in New Salem under a false name—a fact that proved Lincoln right but only after McNamara had left town suddenly. His sudden departure came as a surprise to everyone and devastated Ann. He had received news one day from someone in another town and then disappeared.

It turned out that even some of her close friends were suspicious of him, but she was blinded by her infatuation. Eventually, she faced the truth and came to grips that he was just stringing her along. It broke her heart, and it was said at the time that the disappointment led to her eventual demise.

In her heartbreak, she sought solace in the arms and kindness of Lincoln, who did all he could to nurse her back psychologically to her old self. Some days he made headway, but on other days it was just a backstop to a slide in reverse. But he was patient and read to her when possible, walked with her when she was able, and loved her unconditionally throughout.

Lincoln displayed such powerful empathy during his time with Ann. It was the first time that his highly sensitive personality would be put to good use instead of constantly overwhelming him. This time he could feel what she felt and managed to say the right things to pull her out of it.

She gradually returned to health, and she knew, as did the rest of New Salem, that it was because of Lincoln that she had found a renewed sense of life and a restored faith in love. It was also a side of Lincoln that no one knew or expected from a man so gruff in appearance and so difficult on the eyes. What his external appearance lacked, however, he more than made up for in empathy, kindness, and heart.

He had loved her from the beginning. For her, the love was organic. It developed over time and through the kindness Lincoln had so genuinely expressed and the gratitude Ann so deeply felt. Eventually, she and Lincoln were engaged, and after sufficient time had passed, it was rumored that she found out the truth as to why McNamara had left her—he had a family elsewhere and had returned to them. The final revelation of that news ignited the hurt that Lincoln had managed to quell. The return of the sadness was too much for Ann. This time she descended into such deep depression that her body began to fail. She died not too long after that in 1835 without formally marrying Lincoln.

Her death shattered Lincoln's heart and devastated his mind to an unspeakable degree. He had spent almost four years loving her and pouring his soul into her well-being, and she vanished just as she was beginning to return his love. This event altered Lincoln, who was already in a position that could not understand the loss of those close to him. He had lost his mother and saw the erosion of his father. Then he lost his sister, and the world had turned dark for him. It had made him retreat even further within. It was seeing and getting to know Ann that pulled him out of the depths, and now with her gone, the depths had a stronger pull on him.

In the shadow of her passing, his friends began to worry about him and how quickly he descended into such depression. He lost more weight from an already slender frame. He grew more pale, and he looked and behaved as if he were dead himself.

Things turned bad so fast that close friends worried about his health and even his sanity. It became common knowledge that Lincoln had gone senseless. He could be seen walking about mumbling to himself, totally disheveled and unkempt. He lost his job and began to lose all sense of time and accountability. He even began to run out of money. The Rutledge family was not pressing him to pay for lodging, as they understood his situation and were grateful to him for raising their daughter from the depths.

When things started to get out of hand, a Mr. Bowline Greene, who was a close friend, took him to a secluded location away from things that could remind him of the late Ann Rutledge and saw to his recovery. He spent months by Lincoln's side helping him get back on his feet. In that time, the two grew closer. It was a friendship that Lincoln would never forget, and he deeply appreciated Mr. Greene's efforts in raising him from the pit of despair.

The time away from Rutledge's inn and the familiar surroundings that would remind him of Ann, along with the outdoors and the soothing comfort of a friend, did much to help Lincoln strengthen his mind and put the past behind him, although it deeply altered the state of his psyche. Ann would always be the woman he loved foremost. Even in the White House, he often entertained thoughts of her that would spring up when things took a turn for the worse. It was a bittersweet distraction from some of the dark days of the White House.

Just as he was regaining his hold on life, Mr. Greene, who was instrumental in lifting Lincoln out of his depression, passed away, dealing a severe blow to Lincoln's already fragile state of mind and emotion. It is understandable that by this point Lincoln had started to believe that he was a magnet for bad omens and ill will. There was just so much death around him, and each time the extraction was from within his soul.

Lincoln spent the next few months shuttling between the graves of Mr. Greene and Ms. Rutledge, sobbing at the loss that he felt in his bones.

Chapter 9 - State Legislator

"This is a world of compensations; and he who would be no slave, must consent to have no slave."

Abraham Lincoln, April 6, 1859

Lincoln was a state legislator for four two-year terms starting in 1835. He was elected as a member of the Whig Party, which in itself is startling since all of Illinois was strongly Democratic. The formal naming of the Whig Party by Senator Henry Clay was the same year in which Lincoln won his first election and that saw a changing of the tide in the power that the current party system had in Washington and across the states and the new territories.

Early in his career as a legislator one of the significant acts he pursued was the relocation of the state capital to Springfield. He and other legislators, referred to as the Long Nine (since all of them were extraordinarily tall men), were in favor of moving the capital to a location that was the geographic center of the entire state. This was significant during the time of Lincoln because transportation was not something that we see or think of in today's terms. Today, we can board a flight, catch a train, or drive on interstate highways, state roads, and otherwise well-paved asphalt roads. In 1836, the only means of travel was the use of horse carriages on dirt roads that turned to mud after a heavy downpour.

Travel was arduous, and the need for representatives to travel to and from their constituencies and the need for citizens to come to the capital was a real concern. The idea to move the capital to Springfield signified the clear-eyed nature of Lincoln's view on facilitating democracy.

Springfield grew rapidly once Lincoln had moved the state capital over, and the city was expanding with heavy carriage traffic, shops, fashion, the arts, and entertainment—everything you would expect to find in a growing city. One other aspect of the city was also immigration—not just foreigners coming from Europe but also citizens from neighboring states, such as Kentucky, Indiana, and Virginia.

During the time Lincoln was in the Illinois State Legislature, he was part of a fraternity of pretty raucous reps, but one could never accuse them of being ambitious. It is best to keep in mind that Illinois was not part of the original colonies that formed the United States. Illinois Territory had petitioned the United States federal government to enter the Union and was admitted on December 3, 1818, nine years after Lincoln was born. By the time Lincoln was in the Illinois assembly, it was a body that was merely eighteen years old and fairly inexperienced, but they had vigor and ideals that were obvious from the start. The one core and common fact about the men who won the elections was that they "contained the blood and fire of the frontier." This included such men as Democrat Stephen Douglas, a looming figure in early nineteenth century American politics.

Lincoln's attitude in the assembly was one of seriousness and efficacy. He maintained a silence that implied a reflective and contemplative demeanor, and he didn't take part in any unnecessary ramblings; rather, he continuously observed. In short order, in contrast to the rest of the assembly, his manner was apparent, and the Whigs, who were in the minority, were unanimously looking to him to lead them. They even voted in lockstep to make him Speaker of the assembly. That, however, did not come to pass, as the Democrats were always the majority in the legislature.

During this time, the main concern that occupied the state legislature was the allocation of resources in this newly formed state. There were a significant number of public works projects that were debated and taken up in this frontier state, which was the gateway to opening up the northern part of the Louisiana Territory that stretched from the Gulf of Mexico to the Canadian border.

This was the period when Illinois took up a large amount of debt for its public works. This was common across the colonies and Eastern states. There was significant interest in lending money to the states because they now had the power of taxation, and taxation of the citizens of the state meant that they had a large and predictable revenue base to be able to extend sufficient credit.

In those days, the United States didn't enjoy AAA credit as it does today, and there were no rating agencies to administer those ratings. Instead, you had men acting as financial brokers, such as George Peabody, shuttling back and forth between America and the Old World selling debt instruments at a rapid pace. However, a number of states were inclined to stop payment of interest and eventually cut back on paying back the debt they took on. The main cause for all this was overleveraging state income and the subsequent fall in the economy in the early to mid-1800s. A number of states eventually stopped paying the interest on the notes, and many willingly went into default.

The Europeans, many of whom were the investors in these state papers, lost a large amount of money on the financing of infrastructure projects in the United States, but there were a few exceptions. Many of the states eventually paid up, which included Illinois, and this was done at the behest and insistence of Abraham Lincoln. It may have been late, but the Illinois state government eventually fulfilled its debt obligations after suspending debt payment in 1840. This was done in no small part due to Lincoln's strenuous efforts.

It is rather misguided to think that Lincoln was the kind of person who was laid-back in his magnanimity and silent to the point of being weak. He was neither. His silence was about understanding the opponent, and his desire to be in government was to be able to bring about change and develop the Union beyond what it was at the time while maintaining his puritanical values.

His affinity to the Whigs and his later disappointment with their alteration of principles and his eventual attraction to the new Republican values as outlined by Hannibal Hamlin were not something that he was convinced off or learned to see the virtue in. No. They were the manifestation of the person that he was inside. Take, for instance, the issue with Illinois debt that the governor and the legislature were planning on defaulting on. In that period of debates, Lincoln fought hard to convince the majority party that defaulting was not good for the state and against the moral fiber of the new country. They eventually listened to him and were convinced by his points, and so when the time came, they suspended the payment of interest but eventually paid it off in full. That has Lincoln's nature in its soul.

When Lincoln first arrived at the new state capital in Springfield, he visited a store to prepare for his move for the assembly's sitting. His first stop was to acquire bedding and other related articles. His reputation had preceded him, and they trusted him even before he set foot in the store. He eventually found out that all the things he needed to purchase amounted to $17. He didn't have enough to pay for it; in fact, he had very little money. The store owner instantly agreed to give him all the goods on credit. This caused him grave consternation, which the store owner could see in his face. The point is that it mattered what character the man behind the legislation happened to be. If you have a man who is corrupt, you get a country that follows suit. If you have a man like Lincoln, then you have a state (when he was a legislator) that paid its bills, albeit late.

Along these lines, Lincoln had deep thoughts and ideas on social philosophy, which have been documented by accounts retold by his friends and confidants. Many of his ideas that he formed reading Clay's words and the planks of the Whig Party, as well as from his own experience in law and being in the courts, led to thoughts he would have in the White House. One such thought was the abolition of slavery.

To be clear, you cannot extricate the story of the sixteenth president of the United States from the evolution of slavery without distorting what it is to be America. One must also take into account

Lincoln's age at this point. He was fairly young, and if you could add to that minimal formal schooling on his part, reduced childhood socialization, and the preponderance to read, you will have what we easily label today as being a "nerd." That is in no way being disrespectful to a great man but rather a description of the man who looked beyond the technology and social issues of the day and laid the path of a vibrant future, keeping in mind that what he did was alter the course of the country.

Before being president and as president, Lincoln had two major issues on his mind: (1) his heart and soul were in the unity of the Union, and (2) he believed in the literal meaning of the Declaration of Independence in its broadest interpretation. The notion that all men were created equal by one God struck his Puritan upbringing like a gong, and it was very important to him that slavery was not something that should be part of American values.

Even though the men who were responsible for American independence and the man who wrote the Declaration of Independence were all slave owners themselves, Lincoln was not inclined to define the term "men" in the "All men are created equal" statement as limited to the Pilgrims who arrived by transport vessels and not include the men and women who arrived shackled in slave ships. To him, "all" was absolute, and the idea of slavery vexed him deeply.

The Civil War that was fought right in front of his eyes was not a battle between the North and the South. It was fought because of the two ideals of America that he held to be true and to be great—unity (through the Union) and equality (through the Declaration of Independence). These factors were not inseparable, but it was exactly what was being ripped apart at the seams. Lincoln said,

"All such questions must find lodgment with the most enlightened souls who stamp them with their approval. In God's own time they will be organized into law and thus woven into the fabric of our institutions."

Top this off with being in the state legislature and then becoming a capable lawyer and you see an academic and cerebral side of Lincoln that one almost always forgets after being introduced to his humble and backwoods upbringing. It would be a mistake to discount Lincoln's position on the misconceived notion

In his speech in Peoria, while making his case against the Kansas-Nebraska Act, Lincoln talked at length about the issue of slavery and the manner in which the U.S. Congress had decided early in its history that slavery would not expand beyond the new territories:

"Mr. Jefferson, the author of the Declaration of Independence, and otherwise a chief actor in the revolution; then a delegate in Congress; afterwards twice President; who was, is, and perhaps will continue to be, the most distinguished politician of our history; a Virginian by birth and continued residence, and withal, a slave-holder; conceived the idea of taking that occasion, to prevent slavery ever going into the north-western territory. He prevailed on the Virginia Legislature to adopt his views, and to cede the territory, making the prohibition of slavery therein, a condition of the deed. Congress accepted the cession, with the condition; and in the first Ordinance (which the acts of Congress were then called) for the government of the territory, provided that slavery should never be permitted therein.

Thus, with the author of the Declaration of Independence, the policy of prohibiting slavery in new territory originated. Thus, away back of the constitution, in the pure fresh, free breath of the revolution, the State of Virginia, and the National congress put that policy in practice. Thus, through sixty of the best years of the republic did that policy steadily work to its great and beneficent end. And thus, in those five states, and five million of free, enterprising people, we have before us the rich fruits of this policy . . . But now new light breaks upon us. Now congress declares this ought never to have been; and the like of it, must never be again. The sacred right of self-government is grossly violated by it!"

The point that he was constantly making, and it was not limited to the speech in Peoria (part of which is quoted above) dated October 1854, was that much of the land beyond the original states was to be free, but Congress itself was looking to alter that promise and change the fate of the territories. The issue at hand for Lincoln was not that they originally wanted to change the state of slaves in the original states, but he didn't want to expand slavery into the rapidly westward expanding lands and territories. But that is exactly what Congress was implying in passing the Kansas-Nebraska Act—in direct violation of the Missouri Compromise.

Chapter 10 - Marriage and Life After

It was 1836, and Mary Owens was visiting her sister when Lincoln noticed her. Ms. Owens was previously married to someone who had died some time earlier. Her status now made her eligible for marriage, and the lady's sister had half-jokingly suggested that Lincoln pursue Ms. Owens. In the blink of an eye, it seemed that Lincoln was now engaged, and he half-heartedly pursued her in an obligatory, yet unenthusiastic manner.

It was all an apparent misunderstanding that started off perhaps as a possible wish on the sister's part, but it dragged on excruciatingly until the point when he actually proposed—again, out of obligation—and Ms. Owens politely declined. She later said that it didn't seem possible to have a happy life with Lincoln, even though she did say that he was an intelligent and honest man. She didn't feel that there was, in today's vernacular, any chemistry between them.

The response to her refusal was mixed on Lincoln's part. In letters that were in Lincoln's own hand, he repeatedly gives two distinctly opposing points of view. On the one hand, he expresses relief, and on the other he expresses regret.

This is critically indicative of Lincoln's frame of mind and his character. It is typical in people of conflict like this that there are two parts of him that are in active play. The first part is that he is a person who is highly driven by the right way to do something. Even though he wasn't really interested the relationship, he was dragged along by his own desire to do what seemed to be the right thing.

On the other hand, he was driven by his lack of chemistry, and he was undoubtedly still grieving over Ms. Rutledge. Overall, it was a painful time for him that was a cocktail of events from the time surrounding Ms. Rutledge. That was the recurring theme in Lincoln's life. It's as though there were two sides of him that he needed to resolve, and it always manifested in his earthly life.

The break was saddening but not devastating. It was now 1838, Martin Van Buren, the founder of the Democratic Party, was in the White House, and Lincoln was coming up to his second term in the Illinois State Legislature. One of Lincoln's closest allies in the assembly was a man by the name of Ninian Wirt Edwards. He was the son of the only governor of the Illinois Territory before it became a state. Ninian was married to Elizabeth Porter Todd, Mary Todd's sister.

The Todds were from Kentucky, Lincoln's birthplace. Elizabeth Porter was the first to move to Illinois in search of better prospects, and she was supposed to scout the area and then send word to her younger sister Mary Todd about whether or not she should make the trek northbound. Illinois was a lot better than Kentucky in Elizabeth's assessment, and she invited her sibling to visit.

Mary Todd left Kentucky in 1839 and arrived in Springfield to stay with Elizabeth. Ms. Todd was twenty-one years old at the time and weighed a slender 130 pounds. She was well educated and had a strong family background. The most important aspect about her was that she was an eloquent and unrelenting talker.

Talkers usually get comfortable with silent audiences, and silent people usually feel comfortable in the presence of talkers. And so it was a meeting of well-paired opposites when Lincoln first laid his eyes on her when he visited his friend's home where she was staying.

Initially, Mrs. Edwards had discounted the possibility of any chemistry between Lincoln and her sister, thinking that the pair were not suitable for each other because of their seemingly opposite nature. She liked Lincoln, but she also thought he was a little strange.

It was Mr. Edwards who was looking out for his good friend and thought that it would be interesting to pair him with his wife's sister. Because of Elizabeth's hesitance, the initial meeting between the two was significantly delayed. Elizabeth was looking for better prospects for her sister but to no avail. Of course, in the end, she was proven wrong, but it made the journey that the two of them had to make to each other's orbit that much more difficult.

That was not the only barrier and obstacle between the two. As if by karma, another suitor approached, this time in the form of Stephen Douglas. Mr. Douglas, a fellow legislator and the man who went on to beat Lincoln in the race for senator from Illinois, was also intensely interested in courting Ms. Todd. Elizabeth was a lot more interested in pairing her sister with Mr. Douglas for the typical reason that he was a lot more handsome and seemed to have better career prospects.

By the time Douglas could make any advances on Ms. Todd, Lincoln had already made her acquaintance and was pursuing her affection in the most aggressive and gentlemanly manner possible. Mary reciprocated.

Douglas, nonetheless, made his advances. However, the approach made by Stephen Douglas was a little jarring for Lincoln, and the friction that was already between them deepened. In response, Lincoln decided to withdraw his engagement with Ms. Todd. It was not something that was necessary, but it goes to show the level of Lincoln's feel of inferiority. Lincoln by all counts was someone who had a diminished self-esteem.

The relationship between Lincoln and Douglas was something that was deeper than just two opposing legislators. Douglas was everything that Lincoln had wanted to be. While Lincoln had to fight tooth and nail to get it, Douglas had it handed to him, almost on a silver platter. That was not the sole reason, though, why Lincoln begrudged him. It was also and more so because of the intellectual and moral differences they had. Douglas was a Democrat with slavery as one of his main positions. Douglas had drafted and introduced the Kansas-Nebraska Act, and Lincoln had (long after this association with Ms. Todd had ended) spoken out against it. Their differences came to a head during the Lincoln-

Douglas debates, where they argued their points about the way the country should go forward. One of the strongest lines in his debate was, "He [Stephen Douglas] is blowing out the moral lights around us, when he contends that whoever wants slaves has a right to hold them; that he is penetrating, so far as lies in his power, the human soul, and eradicating the light of reason and the love of liberty, when he is in every possible way preparing the public mind, by his vast influence, for making the institution of slavery perpetual and national."

The debates between Lincoln and Douglas before the Senate election in Illinois was the catapult that shot Lincoln onto the national stage. While ultimately losing to Douglas and seeing him leave for Washington as the senator from Illinois, Lincoln was disappointed. Upon defeat he said,

"The fight must go on. The cause of civil liberty must not be surrendered at the end of one or even, one hundred defeats. Douglas had the ingenuity to be supported in the late contest both as the best means to break down, and to uphold the Slave interest. No ingenuity can keep those antagonistic elements in harmony long. Another explosion will soon come.

"I am glad I made the late race. It gave me a hearing on the great and durable questions of the age, which I could have had in no other way; and though I now sink out of view, and shall be forgotten, I believe I have made some marks which will tell for the cause of civil liberty long after I am gone."

With Douglas making the advances that he was not comfortable with and withdrawing his engagement, Lincoln displayed the character of a man who wanted his failures to be on his say-so and not at the rejection of others. Much of his life felt that it was beyond his control, and many of his losses seemed to be that way. From the time he lost his beloved mother, then his dear sister, and, of course, the loss of his beloved Ann, a lot of what Lincoln felt was the lack of control of his happiness. This is partially the reason why he decided to withdraw his engagement. Upon writing his letter, he showed it to one Joshua Speed.

Joshua Speed was a close friend, and in some later writings has been described as Lincoln's lover, but there is no evidence of this, and at the time homosexuality was not an acceptable lifestyle, yet it did exist in the periphery. A lot of analysis in the post-Lincoln years was rife with this speculation. It drew circumstantial evidence from Lincoln's constant travel away from Mrs. Lincoln and by the stories of the way that Speed and Lincoln shared the same bed for an extended period of time. It must be stated, however, that many men used to share a bed in those days, and it was not always homosexual men. In any case, what we can be certain about is that Lincoln and Speed were very close friends, and he wrote the letter to Ms. Mary Todd intending to break off the relationship.

After writing the letter, he showed it to Joshua Speed, who told him that it would be better from him to approach the recipient in person and that sending a letter by messenger would not be the gentlemanly thing to do. Hearing the thought of appearing ungentlemanly vexed Lincoln, but he decided to talk to her at the first opportunity.

The whole idea of the breakup was really a mixture of misunderstanding and the pressures that he was facing at the end of his second year of his first term in the state legislature. The bills that he had supported in the minority were not going well. His good friend had recently passed away, not to mention Ann Rutledge's recent passing and his most recent rejection from Mary Owens. There was, as you can imagine, much that occupied him.

Ms. Todd cried upon hearing Lincoln's decision to break off the engagement, and so Lincoln kissed her and tried to talk her into feeling better. His way of consoling her really was a way of renewing the engagement—a fact that Speed brought to his attention when Lincoln recounted the events that transpired.

On January 1, 1841, a bridal party assembled, but the groom seemed to be missing. When his friends went to find him, it was as though he was in a state of confusion. It was such a bad state that his friends took turns watching over him and didn't allow him to be alone. It seemed that he was at the cusp of a severe manic-depressive episode.

There is a written record in his own hand of the events of the day in which he writes of "the fatal 1st of January, 1841," and how he had broken down considerably. He writes again to another friend, "Whether I shall ever be better I cannot tell; I awfully forebode I shall not. To remain as I am is impossible. I must die or be better, as it appears to me." In today's psychological terms, he was in such a depressed state that he even seems suicidal.

It was around this time that Speed journeyed with him back to his home in Kentucky, where Speed and his mother nursed Lincoln back to mental stability.

From there on, some time passed, and Lincoln was not in his mentally depressed state any longer. Speed had since married after some pushing on Lincoln's part. His business in law was also progressing well when the path was rejoined with Ms. Todd's. The path that came together wasn't all the fruit of happenstance. There was some external tinkering by a mutual friend.

It was around the time when he gave his speech to the Springfield Washington Temperance Society.

"Although the Temperance cause has been in progress for near twenty years, it is apparent to all, that it is, just now, being crowned with a degree of success, hitherto unparalleled.

"The list of its friends is daily swelled by the additions of fifties, of hundreds, and of thousands. The cause itself seems suddenly transformed from a cold abstract theory, to a living, breathing, active, and powerful chieftain, going forth 'conquering and to conquer.' The citadels of his great adversary are daily being stormed and dismantled; his temple and his altars, where the rites of his idolatrous worship have long been performed, and where human sacrifices have long been wont to be made, are daily desecrated and deserted. The trump of the conqueror's fame is sounding from hill to hill, from sea to sea, and from land to land, and calling millions to his standard at a blast.

"For this new and splendid success, we heartily rejoice. That that success is so much greater now than heretofore, is doubtless owing to rational causes; and if we would have it continue, we shall do well to inquire what those causes are. The warfare heretofore waged against the demon Intemperance, has, somehow or other, been erroneous. Either the champions engaged, or the tactics they adopted have not been the most proper. These champions for the most part have been Preachers, Lawyers, and hired agents. Between these and the mass of mankind, there is a want of approachability, if the term be admissible, partially, at least, fatal to their success. They are supposed to have no sympathy of feeling or interest, with those very persons whom it is their object to convince and persuade.

"And again, it is so common and so easy to ascribe motives to men of these classes, other than those they profess to act upon. The preacher, it is said, advocates temperance because he is a fanatic, and desires a union of the Church and State; the lawyer, from his pride and vanity of hearing himself speak; and the hired agent, for his salary. But when one, who has long been known as a victim of intemperance bursts the fetters that have bound him, and appears before his neighbors 'clothed, and in his right mind,' a redeemed specimen of long-lost humanity, and stands up with tears of joy trembling in his eyes, to tell of the miseries once endured, now to be endured no more forever; of his once naked and starving children, now clad and fed comfortably; of a wife long weighed down with woe, weeping, and a broken heart, now restored to health, happiness, and a renewed affection; and how easily it is all done, once it is resolved to be done; how simple his language, there is a logic, and an eloquence in it, that few, with human feelings, can resist. They cannot say that he desires a union of church and state, for he is not a church member; they cannot say he is vain of hearing himself speak, for his whole demeanor shows he would gladly avoid speaking at all; they cannot say he speaks for pay for he receives none, and asks for none. Nor can his sincerity in any way be doubted; or his sympathy for those he would persuade to imitate his example be denied.

"In my judgment, it is to the battles of this new class of champions that our late success is greatly, perhaps chiefly, owing. But, had the old school champions themselves, been of the most wise selecting, was their system of tactics, the most judicious? It seems to me, it was not. Too much denunciation against dram sellers and dram drinkers was indulged in. This, I think, was both impolitic and unjust. It was impolitic, because, it is not much in the nature of man to be driven to anything; still less to be driven about that which is exclusively his own business; and least of all, where such driving is to be submitted to, at the expense of pecuniary interest, or burning appetite. When the dram-seller and drinker, were incessantly told, not in accents of entreaty and persuasion, diffidently addressed by erring man to an erring brother; but in the thundering tones of anathema and denunciation, with which the lordly Judge often groups together all the crimes of the felon's life, and thrusts them in his face just ere he passes sentence of death upon him, that they were the authors of all the vice and misery and crime in the land; that they were the manufacturers and material of all the thieves and robbers and murderers that infested the earth; that their houses were the workshops of the devil; and that their persons should be shunned by all the good and virtuous, as moral pestilences—I say, when they were told all this, and in this way, it is not wonderful that they were slow, very slow, to acknowledge the truth of such denunciations, and to join the ranks of their denouncers in a hue and cry against themselves.

"To have expected them to do otherwise than they did—to have expected them not to meet denunciation with denunciation, crimination with crimination, and anathema with anathema, was to expect a reversal of human nature, which is God's decree, and never can be reversed. When the conduct of men is designed to be influenced, persuasion, kind, unassuming persuasion, should ever be adopted. It is an old and a true maxim, that a 'drop of honey catches more flies than a gallon of gall.' So with men. If you would win a man to your cause, first convince him that you are his sincere friend. Therein is a drop of honey that catches his heart, which, say what he will, is the great highroad to his reason, and which, when once gained, you will find but little trouble in convincing his judgment of the justice of your cause, if indeed that cause really be a just one. On the contrary, assume to dictate to his judgment, or to command his action, or to mark him as one to be shunned and despised, and he will retreat within himself, close all the avenues to his head and his heart; and though your cause be naked truth itself, transformed to the heaviest lance, harder than steel, and sharper than steel can be made, and though you throw it with more than Herculean force and precision, you shall be no more be able to pierce him, than to penetrate the hard shell of a tortoise with a rye straw.

"Such is man, and so must he be understood by those who would lead him, even to his own best interest.

"On this point, the Washingtonians greatly excel the temperance advocates of former times. Those whom they desire to convince and persuade, are their old friends and companions. They know they are not demons, nor even the worst of men. They know that generally, they are kind, generous, and charitable, even beyond the example of their more staid and sober neighbors. They are practical philanthropists; and they glow with a generous and brotherly zeal, that mere theorizers are incapable of feeling. Benevolence and charity possess their hearts entirely; and out of the abundance of their hearts, their tongues give utterance. 'Love through all their actions runs, and all their words are mild.' In this spirit they speak and act, and in the same, they are heard and regarded. And when such is the temper of the advocate, and such of the audience, no good cause can be unsuccessful.

"But I have said that denunciations against dram-sellers and dram-drinkers are unjust as well as impolitic. Let us see.

"I have not inquired at what period of time the use of intoxicating drinks commenced; nor is it important to know. It is sufficient that to all of us who now inhabit the world, the practice of drinking them, is just as old as the world itself, — that is, we have seen the one, just as long as we have seen the other. When all such of us, as have now reached the years of maturity, first opened our eyes upon the stage of existence, we found intoxicating liquor, recognized by everybody, used by everybody, and repudiated by nobody. It commonly entered into the first draft of the infant, and the last draft of the dying man. From the sideboard of the parson, down to the ragged pocket of the houseless loafer, it was constantly found. Physicians prescribed it in this, that, and the other disease. Government provided it for soldiers and sailors; and to have a rolling or raising, a husking or hoe-down, anywhere about without it, was positively insufferable.

"So too, it was everywhere a respectable article of manufacture and merchandise. The making of it was regarded as an honorable livelihood; and he who could make most, was the most enterprising and respectable. Large and small manufactures of it were everywhere erected, in which all the earthly goods of their owners were invested. Wagons drew it from town to town -- boats bore it from clime to clime, and the winds wafted it from nation to nation; and merchants bought and sold it, by wholesale and retail, with precisely the same feelings, on the part of the seller, buyer, and bystander, as are felt at the selling and buying of flour, beef, bacon, or any other of the real necessaries of life. Universal public opinion not only tolerated, but recognized and adopted its use.

"It is true, that even then, it was known and acknowledged, that many were greatly injured by it; but none seemed to think the injury arose from the use of a bad thing, but from the abuse of a very good thing. The victims of it were pitied, and compassionate, just as now are the heirs of consumption, and other hereditary diseases. Their failing was treated as a misfortune, and not as a crime, or even as a disgrace.

"If, then, what I have been saying be true, is it wonderful, that some should think and act now as all thought and acted twenty years ago? And is it just to assail, contemn, or despise them, for doing so? The universal sense of mankind, on any subject, is an argument, or at least an influence not easily overcome. The success of the argument in favor of the existence of an over-ruling Providence, mainly depends upon that sense; and men ought not, in justice, to be denounced for yielding to it, in any case, or giving it up slowly, especially, where they are backed by interest, fixed habits, or burning appetites.

"Another error, as it seems to me, into which the old reformers fell, was, the position that all habitual drunkards were utterly incorrigible, and therefore, must be turned adrift, and damned without remedy, in order that the grace of temperance might abound to the temperate then, and to all mankind some hundred years thereafter. There is in this something so repugnant to humanity, so uncharitable, so cold-blooded and feelingless, that it never did, nor ever can enlist the enthusiasm of a popular cause. We could not love the man who taught it—we could not hear him with patience. The heart could not throw open its portals to it. The generous man could not adopt it. It could not mix with his blood. It looked so fiendishly selfish, so like throwing fathers and brothers overboard, to lighten the boat for our security—that the noble minded shrank from the manifest meanness of the thing.

"And besides this, the benefits of a reformation to be effected by such a system, were too remote in point of time, to warmly engage many in its behalf. Few can be induced to labor exclusively for posterity; and none will do it enthusiastically. Posterity has done nothing for us; and theorize on it as we may, practically we shall do very little for it, unless we are made to think, we are, at the same time, doing something for ourselves. What an ignorance of human nature does it exhibit, to ask or expect a whole community to rise up and labor for the temporal happiness of others after themselves shall be consigned to the dust, a majority of which community take no pains whatever to secure their own eternal welfare, at a no greater distant day? Great distance, in either time or space, has wonderful power to lull and render quiescent the human mind. Pleasures to be enjoyed, or pains to be endured, after we shall be dead and gone, are but little regarded, even in our own cases, and much less in the cases of others.

"Still, in addition to this, there is something so ludicrous in promises of good, or threats of evil, a great way off, as to render the whole subject with which they are connected, easily turned into ridicule. 'Better lay down that spade you are stealing, Paddy; if you don't you'll pay for it at the day of judgment.' 'Be the powers, if ye'll credit me so long, I'll take another, gist.'

"By the Washingtonians, this system of consigning the habitual drunkard to hopeless ruin, is repudiated. They adopt a more enlarged philanthropy. They go for present as well as future good. They labor for all now living, as well as all hereafter to live. They teach hope to all -- despair to none. As applying to their cause, they deny the doctrine of unpardonable sin. As in Christianity it is taught, so in this they teach, that

'While the lamp holds out to burn, the vilest sinner may return.'

"And, what is a matter of more profound gratulation, they, by experiment upon experiment, and example upon example, prove the maxim to be no less true in the one case than in the other. On every hand we behold those, who but yesterday, were the chief of sinners, now the chief apostles of the cause. Drunken devils are cast out by ones, by sevens, and by legions; and their unfortunate victims, like the poor possessed, who was redeemed from his long and lonely wanderings in the tombs, are publishing to the ends of the earth, how great things have been done for them.

"To these new champions, and this new system of tactics, our late success is mainly owing; and to them we must mainly look for the final consummation. The ball is now rolling gloriously on, and none are so able as they to increase its speed, and its bulk—to add to its momentum, and its magnitude. Even though unlearned in letters, for this task, none are so well educated. To fit them for this work, they have been taught in the true school. They have been in that gulf, from which they would teach others the means of escape. They have passed that prison wall, which others have long declared impassable; and who that has not shall dare to weigh opinions with them, as to the mode of passing.

"But if it be true, as I have insisted, that those who have suffered by intemperance personally, and have reformed, are the most powerful and efficient instruments to push the reformation to ultimate success, it does not follow, that those who have not suffered, have no part left them to perform. Whether or not the world would be vastly benefited by a total and final banishment from it of all intoxicating drinks, seems to me not now an open question. Three-fourths of mankind confess the affirmative with their tongues, and, I believe, all the rest acknowledge it in their hearts.

"Ought any, then, to refuse their aid in doing what the good of the whole demands? Shall he, who cannot do much, be, for that reason, excused if he do nothing? 'But,' says one, 'what good can I do by signing the pledge? I never drink even without signing.' This question has already been asked and answered more than millions of times. Let it be answered once more. For the man suddenly, or in any other way, to break off from the use of drams, who has indulged in them for a long course of years, and until his appetite for them has become ten or a hundred-fold stronger, and more craving, than any natural appetite can be, requires a most powerful moral effort. In such an undertaking, he needs every moral support and influence, that can possibly be brought to his aid, and thrown around him. And not only so; but every moral prop, should be taken from whatever argument might rise in his mind to lure him to his backsliding. When he casts his eyes around him, he should be able to see, all that he respects, all that he admires, and all that [he?] loves, kindly and anxiously pointing him onward; and none beckoning him back, to his former miserable 'wallowing in the mire.'

"But it is said by some, that men will think and act for themselves; that none will disuse spirits or anything else, merely because his neighbors do;

and that moral influence is not that powerful engine contended for. Let us examine this. Let me ask the man who could maintain this position most stiffly, what compensation he will accept to go to church some Sunday and sit during the sermon with his wife's bonnet upon his head? Not a trifle, I'll venture. And why not? There would be nothing irreligious in it: nothing immoral, nothing uncomfortable. Then why not? Is it not because there would be something egregiously unfashionable in it? Then it is the influence of fashion; and what is the influence of fashion, but the influence that other people's actions have [on our own?] actions, the strong inclination each of us feels to do as we see all our neighbors do? Nor is the influence of fashion confined to any particular thing or class of things. It is just as strong on one subject as another. Let us make it as unfashionable to withhold our names from the temperance cause as for husbands to wear their wives' bonnets to church, and instances will be just as rare in the one case as the other.

'But,' say some, 'we are no drunkards; and we shall not acknowledge ourselves such by joining a reformed drunkard's society, whatever our influence might be.' Surely no Christian will adhere to this objection. If they believe, as they profess, that Omnipotence condescended to take on himself the form of sinful man, and, as such, to die an ignominious death for their sakes, surely, they will not refuse submission to the infinitely lesser condescension, for the temporal, and perhaps eternal salvation, of a large, erring, and unfortunate class of their own fellow creatures. Nor is the condescension very great.

"In my judgment, such of us as have never fallen victims, have been spared more by the absence of appetite, than from any mental or moral superiority over those who have. Indeed, I believe, if we take habitual drunkards as a class, their heads and their hearts will bear an advantageous comparison with those of any other class. There seems ever to have been a proneness in the brilliant, and warm-blooded to fall into this vice. The demon of intemperance ever seems to have delighted in sucking the blood of genius and of generosity. What one of us but can call to mind some dear relative, more promising in youth than all his fellows, who has fallen a sacrifice to his rapacity? He ever seems to have gone forth, like the Egyptian angel of death, commissioned to slay if not the first, the fairest born of every family. Shall he now be arrested in his desolating career? In that arrest, all can give aid that will; and who shall be excused that can, and will not? Far around as human breath has ever blown, he keeps our fathers, our brothers, our sons, and our friends, prostrate in the chains of moral death. To all the living everywhere we cry, 'come sound the moral resurrection trump, that these may rise and stand up, an exceeding great army'—'Come from the four winds, O breath! and breathe upon these slain, that they may live.'

"If the relative grandeur of revolutions shall be estimated by the great amount of human misery they alleviate, and the small amount they inflict, then, indeed, will this be the grandest the world shall ever have seen. Of our political revolution of '76, we all are justly proud. It has given us a degree of political freedom, far exceeding that of any other nation of the earth. In it the world has found a solution of the long-mooted problem, as to the capability of man to govern himself. In it was the germ which has vegetated, and still is to grow and expand into the universal liberty of mankind.

"But with all these glorious results, past, present, and to come, it had its evils too. It breathed forth famine, swam in blood and rode in fire; and long, long after, the orphan's cry, and the widow's wail, continued to break the sad silence that ensued. These were the price, the inevitable price, paid for the blessings it bought.

"Turn now, to the temperance revolution. In it, we shall find a stronger bondage broken; a viler slavery, manumitted; a greater tyrant deposed. In it, more of want supplied, more disease healed, more sorrow assuaged. By it no orphans starving, no widows weeping. By it, none wounded in feeling, none injured in interest. Even the dram-maker, and dram seller, will have glided into other occupations so gradually, as never to have felt the change; and will stand ready to join all others in the universal song of gladness.

"And what a noble ally this, to the cause of political freedom. With such an aid, its march cannot fail to be on and on, till every son of earth shall drink in rich fruition, the sorrow quenching draughts of perfect liberty. Happy day, when, all appetites controlled, all poisons subdued, all matter subjected, mind, all conquering mind, shall live and move the monarch of the world. Glorious consummation! Hail fall of Fury! Reign of Reason, all hail!

"And when the victory shall be complete—when there shall be neither a slave nor a drunkard on the earth—how proud the title of that Land, which may truly claim to be the birth-place and the cradle of both those revolutions, that shall have ended in that victory. How nobly distinguished that People, who shall have planted, and nurtured to maturity, both the political and moral freedom of their species.

"This is the one hundred and tenth anniversary of the birth-day of Washington. We are met to celebrate this day. Washington is the mightiest name of earth—long since mightiest in the cause of civil liberty; still mightiest in moral reformation. On that name, an eulogy is expected. It cannot be. To add brightness to the sun, or glory to the name of Washington, is alike impossible. Let none attempt it. In solemn awe pronounce the name, and in its naked deathless splendor, leave it shining on."

All this was still going on while he was pursuing Ms. Todd. His spirits were back up at this point, and in an uncharacteristic display of bravado, he managed to insult another Democratic politician. That man, one Colonel James Shields, challenged him to a duel to the death.

This event can be partially classified as comical and even silly. In an attempt to make nothing of it, Lincoln proposed ridiculous term of engagement to the duel. Eventually, the duel did not happen.

Once this matter resolved itself and no duel was concluded and as the year came to a close, marriage finally entered his stars, and Abraham

Lincoln and Mary Todd spoke their vows on November 4, 1842.

The wedding was conducted in a private house under Episcopalian tradition and custom. It was the first such wedding that the residents of Springfield had witnessed.

At the time, Lincoln was thirty-two, and John Tyler was in the White House after assuming the post on the death of President William Henry Harrison.

It is no big secret that Mrs. Lincoln was a well-read woman with a hot temper. Nonetheless, her inclusion in the picture now was one that altered the magnitude of Lincoln's trajectory. It may have not changed the direction, but it certainly energized it. Mrs. Lincoln had indeed a hard life. On the one hand, she had to contend with the sequential death of her children, and then she had to deal with the assassination of her husband. Finally, her only living son, Robert Todd Lincoln, had to be the one to take her to court to have her pronounced as mentally insane. It was a tragic end, but it was not something that was a surprise in many ways.

Perhaps it was the seeds of this insanity that already occupied her faculties when they were first married and then progressed as the calamities piled on. The irony is that Lincoln and his wife were kindred spirits. Both had a significant burden on their shoulders, and both were mentally distraught, but both had the strength of a hundred men and were able to withstand the pressures that were needed to bring the country together.

It was common knowledge that when Lincoln was a lawyer and needed to travel the circuit of courts, he would find the excuses he needed to not come home when he had off days. He found every excuse to stay away from the home front and from Mrs. Lincoln.

Chapter 11 - Lincoln's Angels & Demons

"Don't interfere with anything in the Constitution. That must be maintained, for it is the only safeguard of our liberties. And not to Democrats alone do I make this appeal, but to all who love these great and true principles."

Abraham Lincoln

It was not polite to discuss one's psychological state in the nineteenth century. It was taken as disparaging and rude. This was a time when psychology was not fully understood or seen as a medical issue. Mental health is no more disparaging today than cancer would be. It is what it is, but by identifying it and understanding it, it makes the discussion more comprehensible.

In Lincoln's case, there were numerous instances and symptoms that pointed to a psychological profile that would explain much of his behavior. There is also credible evidence, eyewitness accounts, and analysis that show that many of his motivations and decisions were made under the cloud of a tumultuous mind.

To understand Lincoln, this mental state must stand front and center. It cannot be swept under the carpet in the hopes of maintaining a legacy that we think should be. Lincoln was one of the most influential presidents in this county, and regardless of whether or not he was battling mental issues will not make that fact any different. What it will do is also highlight that he was strong to overcome them when he needed to and human, just like the rest of us, to succumb to it when he did. Either way, truth deserves the light of day.

To be clear, Lincoln was not crazy or psychotic. He displayed symptoms and consequences of severe depression. His condition is not surprising in hindsight but was not understood or even contemplated in real time. There was a chance that he was genetically predisposed or environmentally disadvantaged because of the frontier circumstances that he faced early in life and because of the almost impoverished childhood that he endured.

These monumentally difficult and extended periods, from what he was born into to the relationship he shared with his father, the losses of those he loved in his family, and the existential difficulties he experienced in his youth, were all depression-inducing events. If Lincoln were alive today, he would be diagnosed clinically depressed. There are many credible anecdotes of his behavior and reports that chronicled his strange behavior in private and often in public. For instance, when he was nominated as the Republican candidate for president, as the crowd jumped in jubilee and euphoria, Lincoln navigated his way to the platform in a sullen and almost dazed way to greet the crowd. His speech that followed was articulate but bereft of any jubilee whatsoever. Eyewitnesses at that nomination event described later that he did not smile easily and would not be able to see the sunlight at noon.

Lincoln's mental state was a dichotomy because he was not always forlorn and sulking. He hated people and to be in their company, but when he was in their midst, the clouds would lift, and he would be charming, articulate, and effective. The people around him would raise his spirits. Once they left and when he was alone again, he would descend into a deeper state of depression.

Whatever he did, the accomplishments he was responsible for, and the energy that he had to do big things, were purely motivated by cognitive discipline. Once he knew what he needed to do, regardless of how he felt, he would apply the energy needed to get it done. In this manner, he was unique. His energy was monumental in its ferocity and exemplary in its tenacity. He would be able to stay up for hours and read the incoming status telegrams from all the front lines of battles. He would still continue to manage and administer other areas of the country while this was happening. It wasn't just the war that he managed. It was the financial and legislative aspects of governing that were critical in his mind.

The power of his discipline and the ability to guide a mind already fraught with pain is nothing short of exemplary. Most people with his level of depression would recoil and retreat into their private space and shut out the world. This is anathema to being the quintessential politician. By virtue of the electoral process, it is necessary for politicians who are people persons to be better suited for the job. Lincoln was not this in the least.

Lincoln was not a natural politician. He was disciplined. When circumstances demanded it, he would be as outgoing and vivacious as the situation demanded but not an ounce more. He was able to go out and engage with people and convince them of any position that he saw to be right or one that would help his cause.

It is highly likely that his depression had a deeper cause. No doubt his environment contributed to it and no doubt his life experience contributed to it as well, but the one thing that explains his susceptibility to it and his ability to read his immediate surroundings well would be that he was deeply empathic. Lincoln had all the earmarks of someone with a high EQ—the measure of the emotional quotient.

In other words, Lincoln had high levels of natural empathy for all things and individuals around him. It is like someone who is highly sensitive to a wide range of frequencies is able to hear sounds the rest of us can't at low volumes the rest of us are unable to. In the same way, high-EQ individuals are sensitive to all things around them. They are able to pick up the slightest hint of things and the nuances of all that is going on. This often renders them overwhelmed and often in tears. Lincoln had that symptom, too, as he was often in tears for things that most people would not give a second thought to.

The opposite side of that same sensitivity manifested in the way he interacted and engaged with people around him and the crowds in the audience. He could pick up on what they were thinking and feeling, and he would be able to read the room well enough to be able to mold his message in a way that they would respond well to.

He was also highly sensitive to the desires of people, and he was able to use his insight to choose his methods and his words to tell them exactly what they wanted to hear to get the result he wanted. Eventually, when he was done with them, they would do as he asked.

His empathy was also able to draw energy from the crowds. Because he could tell them what they wanted to hear and they would feel good about it, that would then infect his demeanor, and he would start to feel good about himself and the way the talk was going. The crowd and President Lincoln would feed off each other.

That engagement energized him and put him on his best footing, but as soon as the back and forth was done and each side went their own way, he could only sustain that euphoria for a moment or two before slumping back down under his dark clouds. On one side of the engagement was the man who was vivacious. On the other side was the sullen and silent man who did not like going out to meet people until he did it. He would prefer to stay alone, read, or just be silent dealing with the demons inside his head.

When that nomination event was over, his friends found him sitting alone in one of the many chairs that were there. He was amidst darkness and the smell akin to a sweaty saloon the morning after a brawl. Lincoln sat there quietly looking even more sullen. His only words to his friends were that he was feeling gravely ill. He was having an episode where depression was racking him from the inside, and he could not bring himself to exit the predicament. This depression only escalated throughout life without any help or natural circumstances to curtail it. The only thing that kept him sane was the discipline to do the right thing for the country as he saw fit.

It was this right thing, that even though the this is in the book diverges from the common wisdom that Lincoln was the emancipator of the slaves and there couldn't have been a racist figure in the makeup of his body and soul, the said thesis wants to paint the picture that is supported by all the facts and not just ones that support a statesman of pristine substrate.

When caught in uncomfortable or stressful predicaments, he would punctuate the time with jokes, inappropriate for the situation, and comments that would elicit laughter from the neighboring crowd and for him. It was one of the ways that he could kick-start any change in his mood. Those were the times when it was easy to understand that things had gone too far, and they went too far too often.

The person he spent the most time with in his life ended up being Mary, his wife. She was also the person who would and could drive him to the deepest depths of his depression. Before their son passed, her tenacity and constant fuel for his ambition would drive him to feel inadequate. After becoming president, she was there to push him in assessing the war in a certain way, but soon after their son passed, her dark clouds only deepened his. Mary was a powerful character and a domineering personality in Lincoln's life.

She was the one person he would never have a cross word with or perpetuate a conflict. Some suggest that his love for her was so deep that he chose to remain silent rather than prove his point just so that it would not hurt her. They would debate, occasionally they would argue, but the times when he would press his point until she acceded were rare.

Mrs. Lincoln was also said to harbor an unstable mind, and Lincoln himself was fully aware of it. It was part of his own burden to carry. Psychologists have been kind in their labeling of Lincoln, calling him chronically melancholy. There is even suggestion that his marriage to Mrs. Lincoln was also a factor in his mental deterioration.

These factors, whatever they were that sparked the depression, ironically, also gave him the strength he needed to endure something as catastrophic and drawn out as the Civil War.

Besides his state, he had a mind-set that was quite different from what we would consider rational thought. This in no way suggests that he wasn't a great president—he was. It is merely drawing a distinction that shows that one's path to greatness is not what one is used to thinking.

Lincoln had displayed a sense of destiny in all his actions. He believed strongly that he was meant to accomplish great things, which he did. This sense of destiny may have also been what countered his melancholy states when they struck and drove him to take action when action was demanded.

If one believed in destiny, it could be said that belief was one of delusion. One could then argue that there is a fine line between delusion and greatness. In Lincoln's case, it seems that his strong moral grounding together with his relentless nature were the combination of qualities that resulted in accomplishment. A sense of destiny is not a delusion. Lincoln was never going to be a regular president or someone who just got to office, administered the country, and left at the end of his term. Lincoln stepped into the office of the presidency with that knowledge, and everything that he attempted was tinged with that mind-set. It was what saved him from his own melancholy.

Lincoln had faced many defeats in his life. There were many political defeats and even more personal defeats. In the time between leaving Congress and deciding to run for the presidency, he felt lost. He had lost his sense of purpose. He thought that jumping back into practicing law would be able to alleviate this hollow and life lacking direction, but law practice was even less invigorating than he had imagined. The last time he had practiced law he was on the upswing. He had gone from store clerk and surveyor to lawyer, so the upswing was positive, but when he left Congress, he went from drafting the law to practicing it, and that was a downswing.

This downswing served to aggravate his depression. The last time he was a lawyer the upswing kept him elevated in mood, and the responsibility of keeping clients counseled kept up his cheer. He was also single at the time, and life hadn't taken such a big bite out of him just yet. This time around he had to see the same work but sitting from a different perch. He missed Washington and the ability to advance himself.

There were three stages to Lincoln's depression. The largest of the three was the state of constant fear he was in. His fear was that of being ridiculed and of not being intelligent. He always carried a chip on his shoulder about not being the man that he imagined he would turn out to be. In actual fact, Lincoln was smarter than the average nineteenth-century American. Not only did he know how to read in a society where literacy rates were so low, but he had also taught himself to read. Not only was he smarter than the average settler, but he was also more hardworking.

Lincoln was also naturally partial to long-term outcomes than to short-term benefits. He could see that he was playing the long game, and he settled in for the slog that it would take to accomplish things that stretched to the horizon. But that compounded the stresses on his mind because he would have to spend motivation on an effort but hardly got paid with the sense of accomplishment until much later. The gratification for the work done took some time to come back, and this resulted in eroding his self-esteem.

As this happened, he learned that he had to put up with it because of his "destiny." In regular minds, the moment self-esteem, a decidedly noncognitive feature of the mind, erodes, the person's motivation diminishes, and objectivity reduces. For people who are highly disciplined, they think their way out to do what they have to do, and then they do it even though all the while they are in a terrible state of mind—sad and melancholy.

The fear component of his depression did not lead down a path that is regularly traversed by most patients of depression. In Lincoln's case, by virtue of wanting to reach his destiny, he used the main aspects of his depression to fuel him on. It is worth noting that there was no classification of depression in the 1850s. If one faced a string of symptoms, the best they could do is to say they fell ill. In the same way, there was no way someone could classify EQ and empathy.

Those who are diagnosed with high EQ or are said to be empathic or have highly sensitive personalities can then understand that the reason why they feel a certain way has an explanation for it, and they can move on with their lives. Even if they are not able to feel at peace, at least they are not racked by questions. Lincoln did not have the benefit of this diagnosis. All he knew was that he felt very strongly about many things, and he could not express them adequately or address them sufficiently to be able to make them go away.

Instead, Lincoln used what he could and learned to sort the chaff from the wheat. This also took tremendous focus, and he was able to do that. His tremendous ability to apply his mind meant that he had to direct a lot of energy to his thinking and his brain in general. It was one of the reasons why he would get tired and move into deeper states of depression. Besides that, he had been malnourished as a child, which had left some permanent damage to his metabolic system.

Energy management for the president was challenging, and the constant fluctuation in energy that his brain received altered his mood and deepened his depression.

A side effect of that—when the brain is insufficiently energized—is a constant state of panic, anxiety, or otherwise a general state of fear. Fear was a constant companion to Lincoln, but it turned out that this was a plus for him.

As mentioned, fear in most people is debilitating, and they eventually end up not doing much. Of course, not all people are like that, and Lincoln was such a person. He would persevere amidst the fear that was palpable in him, which is further proof of his mental discipline.

There were two stages of fear in his life. The first was that he was not good enough. This fear caused him to try harder. This is the same fear that diminished his self-esteem but also powered him. Once he learned to read and read law on his own, he then feared that he would not be able to do more than that. His fear was one that would grip him to the point that he would frequently get panic attacks. To get over that, he then aspired to do something with the law and to become better than he was. Lincoln was the epitome of the man who uses his fear to climb to higher levels of success. Each level he climbed resolved an old fear and then reinstated fear in a new form.

Once he had learned the law and had written the law as a legislator, he then had the fear that he would not be able to do much after retirement. Between this fear and the boredom during his second pass at a law practice, he began to have more ambitious thoughts.

There were low points in his law career. This happened in the first pass (before his time in Congress) and in the second pass (after his time in Congress). His law partner once commented that Lincoln's melancholy was the worst he had ever seen. It was one that was all-consuming. His depression never abated, but he never stopped doing better.

Lincoln had made it a habit to convert his inner demons into his outer angels. He had converted his challenges to wins and pains to accomplishments. This required the second aspect of his mental makeup—the ability to engage. His ability to engage in the individual tasks that needed to be accomplished so that he could get the final outcome of his choice is legendary.

It is not common to consider that one of the greatest presidents of this land, one of four atop Mount Rushmore, and the only president to preside over a civil war in this country, was given to fear. In fact, he may have been the only president in history who was afflicted and almost debilitated by it.

But the story of Lincoln would not be complete if the aspect of his fear were not transmitted, and it would be accurate to leave the story at fear's feet. The real story is that he was a man who overcame that fear, and it was that discipline to overcome the fear and to clear the mind's fog while gripped by that fear that made this man legendary.

Chapter 12 - Spiritual Center

Lincoln understood more than anything else that the job of the presidency was a place of moral leadership. There is certainly a number of administrative duties and responsibilities that it carried, but when it comes down to it, it is a force like no other that can raise the hearts of man to war or thrash it in the ash heap of history.

Lincoln's spirituality intersected with his intellect. His intellect was built by him, not by the private schools and universities back in England. It was founded on and built by his personal reading of the great writings of the time and about great men that preceded him.

He learned to read, and then he learned what to read and whom to read about. One of Lincoln's most profound experiences began with the Christian Bible. As surprising as this may seem, since it was obvious that he was eventually agnostic, he was a child of deep Christian values who had heard so much of the Bible and the incorrect interpretations of it.

He himself was subjected to the incorrect and skewed representations of the Bible. His powers of reasoning eventually shook him out of it. It is more evidence that Lincoln was intelligent enough to be able to think for himself and work things out without being tutored, taught, or influenced. It was a benefit of his inherent silence. He was not influenced by his backwater surroundings.

Not many people have been able to separate themselves from the influence of their environment. This is especially true in the congregation and how the early frontier Christian thinking would have influenced him but didn't because he floated to the top like oil in water. His first experience with the Bible was not pleasant or positive. He didn't understand the intention and the deeper meanings, and he was confused and gravitated away.

In time, his curiosity led him back to the Bible later in life and allowed him to dismantle the pedestrian interpretation of it and come to understand the true nature of its teachings. That second run at it opened his eyes and helped change the trajectory of his life. You can see the difference this made in the way he spoke to the Temperance Society.

Lincoln was not a jovial man, but he did not have a mean streak in him. He was fairly serious and down to earth, but he was thoughtful and kind to those who engaged him in conversation. He also had Stoic characteristics of conversation. He spoke only when spoken to unless he was campaigning. He also did not speak about things he did not know about. Lincoln was the quintessential gentlemen. To a new acquaintance, none of his demons would surface—only the angels they powered inside.

He spent his time observing rather than pontificating. He spent his mind thinking rather than plotting pleasures. He spent his silence in two ways. One was constructive, the other destructive. His destructive side indulged in deep and dark thoughts of peril and pain. It was part of the negative manifestations of his depression that was rooted within him from a very young age. The second was spent in constructive cognition of the nature of things.

The key to traversing the path toward enlightenment is to be able to contemplate the knowledge that is absorbed through books and observation. It takes time to assimilate these thoughts to a point that they are actually beneficial. Taking things literally and not spending any time deciphering only results in taking away the opposite of what is intended.

For an autodidact like Lincoln, he had stumbled upon the greatest gift that was in his arsenal—the ability to make sense of what he observed and what he read without a third-party interpretation of the matter. That made his self-schooling more effective than any of the schooling he could have attended in his youth.

As for his moral grounding, it was based on deep, old-world Christian values. His ancestors who arrived on these shores were Puritans, and his parents were dyed-in-the-wool, hardcore

Baptists. Lincoln himself was not a practicing Christian. Neither was he atheist. He was more agnostic later in life, and, in fact, he had rejected Baptist teachings and local interpretations of its original intent. He also rejected much of any of the church's teachings and thought them misguided and self-serving.

One of his profound speeches on temperance given to the Springfield Washington Temperance Society makes his inner thoughts on religion and piety clear. Here he lays out his thoughts on the matter that was not common in those days and to an extent today. Aside from his speeches, his actions and his letter have shown us his adherence to Calvinism and the doctrine of predestination that affected his thoughts and actions.

An excerpt from his speech to the society is as follows:

"In my judgment, it is to the battles of this new class of champions that our late success is greatly, perhaps chiefly, owing. But, had the old school champions themselves, been of the wisest selecting, was their *system* of tactics, the most judicious? It seems to me, it was not. Too much denunciation against dram sellers and dram drinkers was indulged in. This, I think, was both impolitic and unjust. It was *impolitic,* because, it is not much in the nature of man to be driven to anything; still less to be driven about that which is exclusively his own business; and least of all, where such driving is to be submitted to, at the expense of pecuniary interest, or burning appetite. When the dram-seller and drinker, were incessantly told, not in accents of entreaty and persuasion, diffidently addressed by erring man to an erring brother; but in the thundering tones of anathema and denunciation, with which the lordly Judge often groups together all the crimes of the felon's life, and thrusts them in his face just ere he passes sentence of death upon him, that *they* were the authors of all the vice and misery and crime in the land; that *they* were the manufacturers and material of all the thieves and robbers and murderers that infested the earth; that *their* houses were the workshops of the devil; and that *their persons* should be shunned by all the good and virtuous, as moral pestilences—I say, when they were told all this, and in this way, it is not wonderful that they were slow, *very slow,* to acknowledge the truth of such denunciations, and to join the ranks of their denouncers in a hue and cry against themselves.

"To have expected them to do otherwise than they did—to have expected them not to meet denunciation with denunciation, crimination with crimination, and anathema with anathema, was to expect a reversal of human nature, which is God's decree, and never can be reversed. When the conduct of men is designed to be influenced, *persuasion,* kind, unassuming persuasion, should ever be adopted. It is an old and a true maxim, that a 'drop of honey catches more flies than a gallon of gall.' So with men. If you would win a man to your cause, *first* convince him that you are his sincere friend. Therein is a drop of honey that catches his heart, which, say what he will, is the great highroad to his reason, and which, when once gained, you will find but little trouble in convincing his judgment of the justice of your cause, if indeed that cause really be a just one. On the contrary, assume to dictate to his judgment, or to command his action, or to mark him as one to be shunned and despised, and he will retreat within himself, close all the avenues to his head and his heart; and though your cause be naked truth itself, transformed to the heaviest lance, harder than steel, and sharper than steel can be made, and though you throw it with more than Herculean force and precision, you shall be no more be able to pierce him, than to penetrate the hard shell of a tortoise with a rye straw.

Such is man, and so *must* he be understood by those who would lead him, even to his own best interest."

This was partly to blame for his bouts of depression. Lincoln would fairly often feel that he was destined for greatness, but he was unable to make it to that point. He felt that way after the loss in the Senate race against Stephen Douglas.

In this manner, we can think of him as a fatalist not to the point of being morbid—but he did believe that he would be killed ahead of his time. That feeling of an early death tied into his feeling of destiny for something great that he would achieve. The thought that it was his destiny to die early made him invincible because it happens to be the one thing that saddened him but also propelled him. A man without his acceptance of impending death could not possibly bear the burden of the decisions that needed to be made during the worst war that has ever happened to Americans on American soil.

The Bible alone was just the starting point because it was the document that was most often pointed to when he was a child to lend credibility to his parents' words and to the words of whoever invoked it as their witness. They may not have been accurate, but it was still invoked, and in time he needed to see it for himself. Nonetheless, it was not the only source of his intelligence. In fact, having a thorough misunderstanding of the Bible propelled him to one of the greatest truisms of knowledge acquisition—question everything. Which he did. That was how he learned and accumulated an increasing level of intellect that gradually evolved into wisdom.

It didn't stop there. Lincoln had a list of books that he read and made every endeavor to further read the books or sources that his heroes read as well. For instance, not only would he fill his mind with words written by Jefferson, but he would also go further and read some of the books that Jefferson thought to be important.

Aside from the books that he used to learn to read, books that taught him grammar to write, and the books that he used to learn his math, there was an interesting list of poetry, fiction, and history. Once he learned to read, Lincoln had a voracious appetite for anything that was in print and consumed it all.

There was also an interesting aspect to this. He seemed to have the ability to commit the reading material, verbatim, to memory. Lincoln was known to be able to quote chapter and verse of whatever source material he was referring to and be able to belt out pages of poetry whenever he needed to. Many of the speeches he wrote during campaigns and delivered on stumps could be recited from the teleprompter in his mind. He did have notes in front of him, but he didn't need to refer to them too often. That was his style of delivery. He spoke to the audience, not at them. He felt that it was better to engage them so that he could catch their real-time feedback to his tone and content.

As his readings progressed, he began reading law books and such. Then he also came across the works of Benjamin Franklin, George Washington, John Adams, James Madison, and his favorite, Thomas Jefferson.

The more he read, the more he found that it strengthened his reasoning, his arguments, and his eloquence. He realized that the shortcomings of his life were made right once again by the act of reading and by the diligence that it required.

The mind that began to develop in the shadow of Lincoln's joy of reading was one that was able to find meaning in all things around him and purpose in himself. It increased the power of his psyche and tipped him toward the belief that a truly spiritual center was cultivated by the total removal of the ego.

Within this thinking lay the problem of his reduced self-esteem and his eventual poor self-confidence. This is the discrepancy that many historians find when trying to understand Lincoln. On the one hand, he was highly effective; he was also well read and highly motivated, but he was also silent and depressed. The missing clue to reconcile this inconsistency was his lack of self-esteem coming from the fact that he believed strongly in the demolition of the ego. He believed that would lead to better understanding of the world around him and the nature of the bigger picture. This was one of the most powerful decisions that he made in his personal life, and it paid off.

By relinquishing his ego, he was able to learn more than his inherent environment would have allowed. Most people are the product of their environment, especially the environment they do not actively choose. No one chooses where to be born and to whom to be born to. The chances of doing well increase substantially when one is born into a good neighborhood with affluent parents. The opposite of that is to be born into a poor family with no possibility of education and no contact with the outside world—the way Lincoln had been. Only few rise to the top when they originally come from that situation, and they do that by relinquishing the ego that is painted by false narratives and, more commonly, by fears. While Lincoln himself was racked with fear, the fear he had was about what he could not achieve and what others thought of him if he didn't achieve, but he managed to find his way into the light and pull himself out of meager conditions. His fear was about not amounting to anything and to be left behind by the narrative of history. He was, however, not afraid that he may die trying. In fact, toward the middle of his life, he started to realize that he would one day be killed and had premonitions about that.

Throughout his life, the continuing suppression of his ego made a big difference in how he treated those around him and how he learned from them. In many circumstances, he knew more than those he was listening to, but he still extracted all he could from their perspective. He may have ultimately not executed matters with their advice, but he gave them a platform. The benefit was more his than theirs because in listening to everyone but not being swayed by everyone he was able to make informed decisions. One of his characteristics that became apparent is that whenever he was low on self-esteem, he would not be able to distinguish between his thoughts and the advice he got from his advisors.

Such was the case during the dark days of the Civil War. In that time, it worked against him because the war was something that he was shocked with. While the blood in the mud bothered him, it was the ripping of the fabric of the Union that dominated his concerns. He was afraid that history would forever label him as the man who split the Union, the antipole to men like Washington and Jefferson.

Lincoln may not have been religious, but he understood the tenets of religion and was deeply spiritual. Religion and spirituality can be confusing subjects and mistakenly thought to be interchangeable. In Lincoln's case, religion was about the dogma that needed to be followed, while spirituality was the nature to be godlike. Lincoln chose the latter.

The nature of Lincoln's self-esteem and ego were renewed as his intellect grew. The more he understood the greater scheme of things around him, the more he was humbled. The more he was humbled, the more he learned. The more he learned, his insight grew. This removal of the ego was evidenced by the fact that he would listen to his advisors, generals, and confidants intently in all matters of politics, governing, and war.

The psyche of a man who could take the insults of his own cabinet members and the generals of his armed forces had two overlapping catastrophes dismantle it. The first was the secession. Lincoln took this personally. He was already weakened by low self-esteem.

The second was the war that broke out. He was put in a position to choose between killing men of the Union or preserving the Union. This was a hard decision to make. Having been put in that position wore on him until it was difficult to overcome, and he retreated into a shell.

When he regained his focus, he was able to stand up to the generals, who by this point had hardly any respect for him. He took it all in stride until they crossed the line or went too far. When that happened and he no longer had any use for them, he would discard them unceremoniously.

Thurlow Weed had this to say of Lincoln: "He sees all who go there, hears all they have to say, talks freely with everybody, reads whatever is written to him; but thinks and acts by himself and for himself." This is further magnified by the fact that he had no firm belief in religious providence—only that of destiny. You can see this time and again in the speeches, as in the one referenced above delivered to the Temperance Society. You will also see it in his second inaugural address:

"Both [sides] read the same Bible and pray to the same God, and each invokes His aid against the other. It may seem strange that any men should dare to ask a just God's assistance in wringing their bread from the sweat of other men's faces, but let us judge not, that we be not judged. The prayers of both could not be answered. That of neither has been answered fully. The Almighty has His own purposes."

This character profile created an inevitable tragic ending to an intense man, one who benefited others greatly but was the chief cause of his own unhappiness. Having said that, it must be stressed that there was no hatred between Lincoln and his wife. In fact, on good days, Mrs. Lincoln was an excellent homemaker and the spark that lit the fuse to go after his destiny. Mr. Lincoln's biographer was meticulous in his chronicling of Lincoln's life even to the point of annoying Mrs. Lincoln with matters that did not please her, such as the chronicling of Ms. Rutledge and the level to which it affected her husband.

A good place to start for us has been his law partner's biography of him titled *Herndon's Lincoln*. Herndon is honest, yet admiring of a man who didn't change the landscape of legislation but sought to alter the way men thought of other men, the way we thought of the Constitution, and the way we thought of the

United States. It is safe to say that no man of the street with regular morals and placid wit would have been able to do the job and achieve the results that Lincoln did. It required a little abnormality of mind to be able to perform this abnormally gargantuan task.

In assessing his state, we see that he was a man driven by morals that he understood in the way he understood it. His goal of not creating an affinity to alcohol at a time when alcohol was a commonplace beverage and when the use of time to engage in unproductive matters was acceptable, we see that Lincoln would have none of those. There is no indication that he was allergic or became ill in any way when consuming alcohol, but nonetheless he stayed away from it. We see that his approach to women was one of absolute respect and courtesy. There was nothing about him that degraded or thought less of a woman. In fact, he placed women on a pedestal, and he was honest enough to tell Mary Owens that he would not provide her with a comfortable life but would still like to marry her. He was brutally honest and didn't hide what he thought.

His thinking was neither rash nor typical. His thoughts were based on his ideals, beliefs, and state of mind.

Lincoln was given to silence. In other words, he thought before he spoke, but it was significantly more than that. His silence was more than what one would assume thinking to be. He was a very deep thinker. There are two aspects to his thinking that are worth noting. The first was his ability to focus and direct his conscious thought.

Lincoln's ability to hold a thought from inception to conclusion is legendary. That was a strong ability in and of itself without even thinking about his ability to see things through to completion. It's how he taught himself to read, learn law and how to legislate, and learn to become familiar with political issues. It was also how he stayed strong in trying times. But it wasn't just that. He was able to subject a large amount of his thinking to the subconscious, which is evidenced by his "out of the box" thinking and his ability to spend hours in silence and then coming up with solutions that just were not available to those who think in the conscious mind.

There was definitely a mental issue in the Lincoln family. If you remember how his father Thomas was subjected to the horrific killing of his father (Lincoln's grandfather).

What is not commonly known is that his stepmother told him early in life that he should never decide to become president just in case he was to be assassinated. Either she was psychic or this was all really a self-fulfilling prophecy on Lincoln's part after being planted with the seed of death early in life. It is reasonable to think that Lincoln had already been planted with the seed long before he was married, and his wife's mental issues were part of his.

Lincoln read extensively. Not as much as Jefferson, but they indeed had some common reading material between them. Among Lincoln's reading list that formed part of his character and gave credence to a soul that was in search of spirituality was a list of books that stood as the foundation of a learned mind.

Lincoln needed to understand the basis of slavery if he was to understand the point that Jefferson was making and what the other Founding Fathers were trying to implement during the genesis of the country. For this Lincoln took the essays of Leonard Bacon on slavery as his primer and his guide. Leonard Bacon was a pastor in the North. He had eloquently written about slavery and balanced the writings with his view on abolition.

Chapter 13 - National Politics

"All this talk about the dissolution of the Union is humbug -- nothing but folly. We WON'T dissolve the Union, and you SHAN'T."

Abraham Lincoln, July 23, 1856

At the end of his fourth term in the Illinois Assembly, Lincoln had decided not to run for any other office at the state level. He had started to set his sights at the federal level and believed that he would be able to extend his calling and do a good job for the people of Illinois and those in the expanding United States.

While he planned his national strategy, he had a family to take care of, so he pursued his law career, partially to put food on the table and also because he enjoyed the career.

In 1846, he stood for and won the seat from Illinois to the U.S. House of Representatives. It was his first and last term in Washington as a congressman, and while his accomplishments may be slight, it gave him a good introduction to national politics. His seat was under the banner of the Whig Party, and it came at a time when the embers of war were being lit at the southern border with Mexico over the annexation of Texas. Lincoln opposed the war and the whole idea of the annexation that was designed by the White House.

This was a highly unpopular view. Much of the nation and the politicians in Washington supported it, while Lincoln kept voting against every vote that came up in the House that had anything to do with the Mexican-American War.

The problem he had with waging the war in the annexation process and the way that the war was sparked put him on the opposite side of most of the country. This was not the first time that he had taken a position that was different from the majority, and being that he was still in the Whig

Party, who were themselves in the minority, his views were not accepted.

The one thing about him that everyone still agreed upon was that he was honest, and his honesty never came into question. That may have even worked against him because they knew that he was standing on the point against the Mexican-American War, and that it was a position that he truly believed in. That could then mean just one thing. It was misunderstood that his opposition to the Mexican-American War was rooted in diminished patriotism. This was not true.

Lincoln accused President Polk of deception in waging war against Mexico as can be seen in his address to Congress excerpted below,

"The President, in his first war message of May 1846, declares that the soil was ours on which hostilities were commenced by Mexico; and he repeats that declaration, almost in the same language, in each successive annual message, thus showing that he esteems that point, a highly essential one. In the importance of that point, I entirely agree with the President. To my judgment, it is the very point, upon which he should be justified, or condemned. In his message of December 1846, it seems to have occurred to him, as is certainly true, that title—ownership—to soil, or anything else, is not a simple fact; but is a conclusion following one or more simple facts; and that it was incumbent upon him, to present the facts, from which he concluded, the soil was ours, on which the first blood of the war was shed. Accordingly, a little below the middle of page twelve in the message last referred to, he enters upon that task; forming an issue, and introducing testimony, extending the whole, to a little below the middle of page fourteen. Now I propose to try to show, that the whole of this—issue and evidence—is, from beginning to end, the sheerest deception."

This was not the first or the last time that he had expressed this opinion, and it started to become a thorn in everyone's side. It even got to the point that his biographer, whom we have quoted and used as research for this book many times, one Mr. William Herndon, who was also his law partner and close friend, eventually turned on him over the issue. Lincoln was very much alone on this matter except for some support of the Whig Party.

He took on the nickname "Spotty Lincoln" when he demanded to know exactly how the war had begun. It was important to him because he suspected that President Polk had engaged in underhanded tactics in sparking the war. No doubt General Zachary Taylor had done well in the war and was regaled as a hero on his return only to be eventually elected as president, but Lincoln doubted the conditions that resulted in the war that conveniently saw the Union win.

It turns out that Polk was a shrewd battle planner and had instructed Taylor to position his forces in a way that pinned the Mexican army. In their panic and stress, they misunderstood the intentions of General Taylor's camped army and attacked. This was enough reason for President Polk to wage a full-scale battle that was key in the annexation and eventual inclusion of Texas into the United States.

Lincoln eventually goes on to hint that President Polk is dishonest. He said to Congress,

"I am now through the whole of the President's evidence; and it is a singular fact, that if anyone should declare the President sent the army into the midst of a settlement of Mexican people, who had never submitted, by consent or by force to the authority of Texas or of the United States, and that there, and thereby, the first blood of the war was shed, there is not one word in all the President has said which would either admit or deny the declaration. In this strange omission chiefly consists the deception of the President's evidence-an omission which, it does seem to me, could scarcely have occurred but by design. My way of living leads me to be about the courts of justice; and there I have sometimes seen a good lawyer, struggling for his client's neck, in a desperate case, employing every artifice to work round, befog, and cover up with many words some point arising in the case, which he dared not admit, and yet could not deny. Party bias may help to make it appear so; but, with all the allowance I can make for such bias, it still does appear to me that just such, and from just such necessity, is the President's struggle in this case."

The more he pressed his point, the more Congress and the political elite of Washington at the time began to gravitate away from him. Eventually, Lincoln's term in office was up, and he had already decided not to run for a second term. He returned to Springfield, where Mrs. Lincoln and the children awaited his return. But he didn't return right away. He remained in Washington for a few months. Some say that his previous reason for not returning home due to Mrs. Lincoln's treatment of him caused him to stay away this time. That could be, but there was also another reason. He was doing his best to campaign for the presidency of Zachary Taylor, the general who had triumphantly won the Mexican-American War.

In his own words, Lincoln was trying to protect as much of the Wilmot Proviso as he could and not have the incoming president veto it. He was afraid that Taylor's Democratic opponent would step over the Wilmot Proviso and to them, even not knowing that Taylor would or wouldn't, he still took the gamble that Taylor would not, and so he fully supported Taylor. Besides, Taylor was of the same party as Lincoln at the time. He was the last Whig to ever become president and the last Southerner until 1912.

The conundrum was palatable since the Mexican-American War was something Lincoln had not supported and in fact was part of the reason why he had been all but ostracized in the capital.

With that, his stint in Washington ended, and after campaigning for Taylor, he left on a tour of the Northeastern states in what was labeled as a speaking tour. In some sectors of historical analysis, it was deemed that this was Lincoln's version of a listening tour. Instead, it was a prelude to his candidacy for higher office.

That was the first time he went on a speaking tour in New England. It was 1848, and after the tour he returned to Springfield and continued to develop his law practice. He was eventually admitted to the bar and the Supreme Court in 1849.

During his time in Springfield, he kept himself occupied with numerous endeavors of the law, and it is also when he designed and patented his design for the flatboat, which we referred to earlier in the book. (It was U.S. patent No. 6469A.)

The United States was a hot bed of activity as all this was happening to Lincoln. The territories in the West were rapidly opening up, and Lincoln was offered the governorship of the Oregon territory. The Oregon treaty had just been signed with the British three years earlier, and President Zachary Taylor had seen fit to offer the governorship to Lincoln. By this point, Lincoln's views on slavery and their place in the U.S. Constitution was growing significantly stronger, and he wanted to pursue that route instead of heading out west to a new territory. He declined the offer.

The following year in 1850 Lincoln's third son, William Wallace, was born on December 21. Lincoln was exhilarated and stayed home during the few days after the birth to look after his new son. The tragedy that ensued, however, when William was eleven years old and living with Lincoln in the White House was one that hit too close to home for him.

His son died from typhoid fever in February 1862 just a year after the Lincoln family had moved into the White House and less than a year since the Civil War had begun. The link between William's death and the Civil War was the dagger that pierced Lincoln's heart so deep. The Northern army was camped by the Potomac River not far from where the White House drew its water. The contamination from the encamped horses and men (from the waste that washed into the river) had contaminated the water to such a high degree that it caused the infection in young William.

After William's birth in Springfield, Lincoln continued working as a lawyer, traveling around the state and the country. He brought two cases to the U.S. Supreme Court between 1849 and 1852. The first was Longworth vs. Lewis, and the second was Williamson vs. Barrett.

By the time 1853 rolled around, Mrs. Lincoln was pregnant again and gave birth to their third son, Thomas Lincoln, who later died in 1871 at the age of eighteen possibly from cancer, but it is not conclusively known. He died after his father was assassinated, but before his mother was institutionalized.

By 1854, members of the Whig Party had begun to meet regularly looking for a new platform. Lincoln was among these men who were all in favor of creating a new national platform that could take up the expansion of slavery issue and advance it. The best vehicle to do that in politics was through the party mechanism, and since the Whigs were losing out in popularity and the Democrats were advancing, the antislavery Whigs decided that it was time to fire up a new party, so they began meeting, and in 1854 the Republican Party was born. It was March, and Northern Democrat Franklin Pierce was in the White House. By May, the Kansas-Nebraska Bill had been signed into law. It was the spark that lit a fire in Lincoln's soul. If he had any machinations for higher office before, they paled in comparison to this bill coming into effect.

Instead of considering the presidency, he decided to return to Washington as a senator from Illinois and threw his hat into the race. Lincoln stood as a member of the newly formed Republican Party against the incumbent Illinois senator, Stephen Douglas. Unlike today's elections for the Senate, the senators in Lincoln's time were chosen and voted on by the state's assembly. In Illinois, Lincoln would have had to be chosen by his former colleagues at the Illinois Assembly to be able to represent the state in the Senate.

On the national stage Lincoln was hardly known at this time, but he was known well enough at the assembly, and he had a good chance of winning the election. Douglas, on the other hand, had been a rising star in national politics and had wide name recognition. In the runup to the November election in 1858, they conducted a series of nine debates held in nine constituencies across Illinois. It's good to remember that there were no televised debates back then, and the debates allowed a great number of people to attend and the newspapers in those areas to carry the substance of the debate.

The nine debates came to be known as The Great Debates of 1858 or as we have also come to know them as the Lincoln-Douglas debates. Lincoln pretty much knew that he wouldn't have a chance to win because most of the State Assembly consisted of Democrats. It was good, though, that he participated, which centered around the issue of slavery and its expansion into the new territories. This is where the famous line was uttered during the debates:

"That is the issue that will continue in this country when these poor tongues of Judge Douglas and myself shall be silent. It is the eternal struggle between these two principles—right and wrong—throughout the world. They are the two principles that have stood face-to-face from the beginning of time, and will ever continue to struggle. The one is the common right of humanity and the other the divine right of kings."

He ultimately lost the contest, and Stephen Douglas was sent back to Washington as the senator from Illinois, but the debates raised Lincoln's profile from a veritable unknown to becoming a force of the North. His position on slavery and its expansion became the soul of the Northern cause, and his vehemence and resolve became the bane of the South.

It was only on a speaking tour that he stopped at New York's Cooper Union. His speech at the Union was deliberate and hard hitting. It was aimed at three specific groups, and it hit its mark effectively and masterfully. By this point, Lincoln had brushed up his skills as a master orator, and he eloquently targeted the people of the Northeast, the people of the South, and to the new part of the Republicans.

After the Lincoln-Douglas debates ended, Stephen Douglas returned to Washington, and Lincoln did not know what to do next. It was the second time that he had lost an attempt to get to the Senate. It was Mary Lincoln that prompted Lincoln to aim higher and not give up. Much has been written about Mary Ann Todd Lincoln most of which is unappealing and abrasive. But that is to be expected if you consider that she had been through more than her share of suffering and was expected to keep her grace under the scrutiny of the Washington elite when she first entered the White House. It is important to remember that she was a daughter of the South that fully and wholeheartedly supported her husband's views. But her loyalty to the Northern cause was always suspect because of her Southern heritage.

She was well aware that her husband was more than just a simple backwoods man, and she supported him even before they got married. It broke her heart when he had broken off the engagement, and it broke her heart again when he didn't show up for the wedding on January 1, but all was forgiven, and she was the energy behind his solitude and perseverance.

Chapter 14 - Politician

For as difficult a life that he had endured in the early part of his life, Lincoln had managed to emerge into the public eye with the sense and instinct of the consummate politician. In private, his thoughts would lead into darkness, but being in public would alter the landscape of his mind.

Lincoln used the energy of the people around him to transform his inner demons and elevate his persona to something that was larger than life. He did not plan on doing this, but it was a skill that came naturally as the forces in his life molded his fate.

In that respect, Lincoln was a product of his time and place. It was a time of emerging differences that swelled in the subterranean minds of the once-colonies-now-country, where the freedom of all was the force that pulled at the seams of a country stitched with high ideals but a weak understanding of morals.

The central moral issue at the time was not just about the slavery of men, women, and children, but the moral issue that plagued the country was a little more sophisticated than that, and it was plain and clear to Lincoln's mind.

The central moral issue was about the treatment of mankind over the greed for profit. What Lincoln clearly understood and stood against was the manner in which the fabric of morality was being frayed by greed and indifference to human life.

On Lincoln's part, there was the element of political calculation that drove many of his decisions and much of his thinking. It came naturally to him—a chameleon in the truest sense of political adaptability.

While moral outrage powered his heart, political instinct drove his actions. He knew when to speak truth to power and when to pour bespoke honey into the ears of the electorate.

This was on top of his natural linguistic ability that infused his speeches and colored his writing with poetry— poetry that projected the soul of his ideals and the consistency of his intent. This translated into a quality of trustworthiness that vibrated in the timbre of his voice and resonated in the hearts of his audience. It was hard to dislike this awkwardly tall man with a face seemingly chiseled by an unskilled carpenter.

During one of his campaigns for elected office, as he was making his case to the attendees, a fight broke out amidst the crowd between two men diametrically opposed on some topic.

Lincoln halted, jumped off the podium, and briskly made his way to the ongoing fisticuffs. Upon arriving, he effortlessly pulled the two men apart and cross-examined them as to the cause. It turned out that the men disagreed with each other about the topic of Lincoln's speech. One was in Lincoln's corner, the other decidedly on the other side.

By the time Lincoln was done with both, he had gained a new supporter. In his brief contact with these men, he had managed to pour that honey potion he was so famous for and warmed the hearts of both, the advocate and his antagonist. If only Lincoln were able to speak to every person in the South like that the immorality of racism and stain of slavery would have been omitted from the tomes of American history.

Lincoln's fabric as a politician was a complex weave of personal trials and sufferings, with the interest in the academic approach to better understanding. As much as Lincoln strove to learn, it was not the academics that interested him. It was the development of the mind and the assimilation of knowledge that animated his actions.

Understanding this point is crucial for understanding Lincoln and the shape of his mind. In the mid-nineteenth century, there were a small number of grade schools, even fewer high schools, and only a handful of institutions of higher learning. Not only was it cost-prohibitive to attend school, but the closest one could sometimes be half a day's walk, which made it impractical to attend, especially since there was a mountain of chores to help with at home or on the farm.

There were other reasons beyond cost and convenience as well. It was sometime a matter of opportunity cost. Even if the schoolhouse was next door and there were no chores to attend to, the time at school took away from being at a job to earn that extra penny that helped put food on the table.

Going to school helped in learning some math, reading, and writing. Everything else was geared at being able to get a job in the future. Being a farmer didn't need that. It wasn't until just after Lincoln's time did the idea and concept of academic advancement enter the mainstream.

Without the systemic pressure of getting an education or at the very least to be part of the paper chase, boys grew into men without the benefit of organized learning. Each was left to his own devices to put food on the table in any way they could.

Lincoln had undergone all of this at this time. There was no need for an education. He just needed to paddle his barge, handle a saw, and make change behind the cash register. Yet, his interest in language catapulted his ability to communicate, his ability fueled his desire to improve himself, and his desire traced his arc across history. He was truly self-made.

The backdrop to all this was the pain that colored his thoughts. In his metamorphosis from frontiersman to politician, he still lived a life trapped by many of the same responsibilities that all young adults had. Despite the challenges, he found the time and the will to advance his reading, develop his grammar, and perfect his communication before he picked up a copy of the Illinois constitution and the subsequent law books that put him on track to understand the law. This was the beginning of a life that would pit career against morals. It was the spark that lit the awareness that not all laws were just.

They say that a man is the vessel that contains the sum of his past and his vision of the future. In Lincoln's vessel, the two were diametrically opposed. One was dark, the other enlightened.

However lofty his ideals, it is only fair to remember that Lincoln was the quintessential politician. The honey potion he trickled into the ears of his audience was made of one part poetry, three parts hyperbole. He was still, nonetheless, Honest Abe. The sobriquet reflected the measure of his moral vessel without mitigating it by how easily he bent the truth in exchange for a ballot.

A competitive streak navigated aggressively within the shadows of Lincoln's intellect. He was not a man who would be bested by a situation or a person. He did whatever he needed to do and went wherever he wanted to be—and he was relentless.

That same inherent tenacity saved him from his own demons later in life when he transitioned from politician to statesman.

His first presidential campaign was won by a fluke. The gods were smiling on him, and the three other candidates split the popular vote to give him the Electoral College, but it was not always like that when he ran for Congress.

He made it a point to canvass the constituencies and speak with hordes of constituents over the course of the campaign no matter how far-flung the travel to do so. He would win super majorities of the votes. In one instance, he won 297 out of 300 possible votes. He was dogged in his campaigns and took time to talk to each man, woman, and child about the issues that plagued them and offered a consoling word to whatever their plight may have been. Politics was indeed a calling for young Abe.

America is a land of laws. It always has been since its inception. Founded on the word of a consensus between thirteen states in 1776 and articulated in Jefferson's Declaration of Independence, it was an aspiration cast in the desire of a perfect union and bound together by the toil of men.

Those words that gave rise to a country of laws, which brought forth a nation of diversity that became the bastion of freedom and prosperity, were rooted in righteous morality.

So it was apt then when the nation found itself standing at a moral fork in history, that providence dispatched a man of righteous fabric fluent in the law and steeped in political instinct to shepherd it.

The individual, the country, and the shepherd were all presented with a choice. The choice, rarely presented as binary, was fortunately so this time. It was only the second time in this experiment of self-governance that the soul of the collective was asked to choose. It was not merely a choice between slavery and abolition, white and black, rich and poor. It was, plainly and simply, about good and evil.

To be clear, all that is not righteous cannot be deemed evil until a point comes in the unfolding of events where equity, humanity, and civility are forsaken. Such was the case in the years leading up to the Civil War.

Each person had to look within, the country had to make its choice, and Lincoln had to find the strength to vanquish evil simply by doing what was right regardless of the cost.

As history unfolded from the Potomac to the Mississippi River, it became painfully clear to Lincoln that it was no longer just about the law, the vision of the Founding Fathers, and the economic foundations of the country. He realized that it was about the battle for the moral fabric of the country and its future.

That was the choice that faced Lincoln, but it was wrapped in a complex web of externalities. When it is a simple choice between good and bad or when it is a clear-cut issue, most Americans do the right thing. But when the issue is wrapped in layers of interconnected issues and prejudices, self-serving circumstances, and personal hardships, it does not just become difficult to choose right from wrong. It becomes hard to even see what is right.

What started out as an imperative to survive, with memories fresh of how countless families lost farms or worked themselves to the bone, there was a string of hardworking men and women who needed farmhands to work the farm that they owned or would be unable to feed their families. There were large plantations owned by wealthy families and who would not be able to be price competitive or worth the full extent of the farm without the slave labor they had. More importantly, most of the poorer farmers or less substantial plantation owners always carried a large debt to the slave traders. If they lost the slaves, they would owe money to the traders and not have enough hands to work the farms to pay down that debt. They could be out on the street. The problem was systemic. None of this is to excuse the morality of the situation but to

There was another problem as well. By the time Lincoln was born in 1809, indentured servitude had evolved into outright slavery and been that way for two centuries. The practice had spread wide across the land and deep into the culture of the colonies. The burden of the path slavery took lies partially on the shoulders of the slave trade industry. Slavery did not happen overnight.

Beyond the surface of the visual suffering, which was horrendous in its own way, there was a more fundamental and painful issue that drove the minds of those who endured it and understood the consequences. A country that acquiesced to the temptation to corrupt the soul would have been forever damned.

The battle between forces of freedom and of slavery, dignity and greed, North and South was all that and more. It was, in final measure, about the fundamental matter of seeing God in all man—something that had long been forgotten as the desire for a strong labor force powered the personal economy and fueled national growth.

Lincoln was a figure of the nineteenth century. Born in 1809 and assassinated in 1865, he was of a generation that emerged from the pivotal years of the eighteenth century—a consequential chapter in the country's history to say the least. It saw the gelling of a new nation, from many, one, and the battle for independence. It also saw the aggressive ramping up of industry. In the eighteenth century alone, an estimated eight million new slaves were brought into the country. The average price of a slave was $2,000 in the year 1750. In today's dollars, that's about $80,000. With eight million brought in, that makes the slave industry worth $640 billion between 1700 and 1800. That's an average of $6.4 billion a year. From a quantitative economic perspective, applying the relevant multipliers, it is sufficed to say that the direct implication of slavery was that it injected billions into the economy. But that is just the revenue that the traders make.

The real value in slavery came from a workforce that generated 80 percent of the GDP. Drilling down, the GDP in the North needed fewer slaves and had a cost-competitive position because of the prevalence of mechanization. In the South, the percentage of GDP propelled by slave-heavy industry was higher, and the cost distribution was more toward the slave than any mechanization. Industries in the South were not given to the mechanical advancements of the day and were still very much dependent on manual labor.

Slavery became the engine of the South. Without slaves, every single farm, every single farmer, and the entire economy that had been built on the back of slaves would collapse. Freeing the slaves meant losing their investment and possibly their farms and livelihood. They could not see past their own fear of hardship in the absence of slavery.

That fear propelled much of the South toward self-preservation. Consequently, as most politicians do, they capitalized on that fear.

There are two rails slavers relied on in their defense. The first was that they did not treat slaves poorly. The second platitude was that they were better off on the farm in America than they were in the village they came from. None of these, of course, were even remotely true, but the point is not if it's true but the mind-set of the slaver. It was a deep and ingrained mind-set that pervaded the colonies and the states. They didn't see themselves as slavers of an entire race of people but as liberators. It was further fueled by the politicians and their fear-mongering.

The first time Lincoln saw a slave auction the indignity of the event overwhelmed him. His perspective of the institution of slavery was not influenced by growing up with slaves, which served to effectively desensitize the heart to the plight of indignity. He and his family had always worked their spread by themselves, and he had gone on to work for others or managed his own business.

Layered on top of this was his strict interpretation of the Constitution and the Declaration of Independence. He learned and resonated with the truism made famous in Jefferson's Declaration that "all men are created equal." His sense of morality, predating his introduction to the document, combined with his intellectual development in the law cemented the character of a man and the integrity of a future statesman.

It was unshakable. Nonetheless, being steadfast in one's morals is one thing, but moving the deep mind-set of a country toward something that goes against their self-interest is altogether different. Had it not been for the Civil War, would the issue of slavery been justly and sufficiently addressed?

Chapter 15 - Electoral Math

In the days after the 2016 election, the topic of electoral math, popular vote counts, and the Electoral College came to the forefront of national politics. It remains obvious that before that election most citizens were not fully knowledgeable or consciously aware that the greatest democracy on earth had a very undemocratic way of electing the president.

It was consequential in 2016, and it was consequential in 1860. Everyone today knows that governing such a sprawling and populous country is complex. Having it as a democracy is even more so because there are many different layers of officeholders at the county, state and national levels. The framers of the Constitution wanted to distribute the levers of control in such a way that every center of power would be able to hold another center of power in check. They wanted to make sure that they steered away from the monarchical concentration of power in both the absolute sense, where the power was vested by convention or legacy, and in the practical sense, where one office gained so much power that the other branches of government slid into obsequious acquiescence.

To keep the powers fragmented and distributed, the elected offices were decided to be performed differently. Each district was given one representative who would go to Washington to voice the concerns of that small group of people. The counties would also elect a representative to the state capital. That state legislature would then choose two people to be senators who would go to Washington to form the Senate. Each state would get two regardless of population. Note that U.S. senators today are elected in a statewide contest instead of being chosen by the state legislature as was the case in Lincoln's time.

To isolate the momentary popularity of the time, elections were staggered. Representatives were elected every two years, while senators were elected every six. That means a momentary sense of appreciation of a party or the hatred of the same would not mean that the diversity of the office bearers would be wiped away in a whim. The Founding Fathers were cognizant of keeping the "whim" factor out of governing politics.

Then, of course, is the factor of the presidential contest, which is held every four years. The difference is that the president is not elected in the same way as the representatives of the Senate. The president is elected by the Electoral College.

This is where the confusion lies and where there is a misunderstanding of how American elections work. The framers decided that the president, who has a pivotal responsibility in the administration of the country and the deployment of its assets, is not directly elected by the people of the country. They are elected by a special group of people that number the same (almost) as the number of representatives to the U.S. Congress in that state. For instance, if State A has twelve representatives in Congress and two in the Senate, then it has fourteen Electoral College votes, but the persons in the Electoral

College are different from the people who were elected to Congress or the Senate. It is these people in the Electoral College who would cast their vote for who becomes president.

It is common fallacy among today's electorate that the Electoral College must go to the popular vote in the state. That is not so in almost half the states. The Electoral College in many states is not compelled by law or the Constitution to vote in the same way as the will of the people in that state. In other words, Candidate X could get fewer of the counted ballots voting in his favor, and the Electoral College could still give all the votes to the candidate it chooses.

That's in the worst-case scenario.

But on the other hand, the way it actually works is that the Electoral College casts its vote according to the will of the people of that state. Whoever gets the majority of the vote, even by one, gets all of the Electoral College votes (in all but two states currently).

The key to understand here is that the majority of the vote does not mean the will of the people. In a straight fight where 100 percent of the constituents vote for one other the other candidate, then someone is going to get more than 50 percent of the vote (as little as 50 percent + 1). But what happens when there are four candidates? That would mean (hypothetically) that if two candidates get exactly 25 percent, then one of the candidates only needs to get 25 percent + 1 of the vote to beat the fourth candidate and collect all the Electoral College votes.

A candidate could ostensibly win 100 percent of the Electoral College by winning a little over a quarter of the state's votes. That is by no means the will of the people.

In the case of Lincoln's first-term election, that is approximately what happened. Lincoln was not the favorite to win. He was a latecomer into the Republican convention, while the favored to win at the time was Hannibal Hamlin, but by virtue of smart politicking on the part of the Lincoln's campaign manager, Lincoln catapulted to the head of the line and scooped up the nomination. Hamlin got the second most number of votes. In the early days of the Union, the vice-presidential candidate for the ticket was chosen by the vote tally. The one with the most votes got the nod for the top of the ticket, while the second got the nod for the vice presidency.

Hamlin was the true champion of the slavery question. He wanted the Republican Party to be the champion for this cause, but this clashed with Lincoln's ultimate goal. It is one for the reasons why Lincoln did not support Hamlin for his second term. It was Hamlin who had the support of the radical arm of the Republican Party.

The Republican Party had split in the middle of Lincoln's first term since the war was going poorly. The Radical Republicans who had full support of the liberal North wanted to distance themselves from Lincoln and his losing war effort. It was also the reason why he had received such criticism from the publications that were Northern liberal in nature.

The personal relationship between Lincoln and Hamlin was also fraught. There were frequent outbursts and friction between them. Hamlin always believed that Lincoln was not doing enough to set the question of slavery to rest. Lincoln had always used the issue of slavery to his benefit but was really looking to consolidate the power of the federal government instead of emancipating the slaves.

By the time the Republican Convention occurred, the party had split, and the Radical Republicans had nominated their own presidential candidate. Lincoln had chosen to take on Andrew Johnson, a war Democrat, to be able to shore up a wider base.

Between the nomination of 1864 and the election at the end of that year, the tide of losses had been stemmed, and the fortunes of the Union effort had turned. And along with it the popularity of a war president who was now winning. The Radical Republican candidate then stepped down and endorsed Lincoln for a second term, who then went on to win the election that November.

There are a number of issues regarding Lincoln's term as president. It must be noted that the effort that is being put into bringing to light that he was not the great Emancipation president is not to disparage his name but to set the record straight that his intention was to unite the country first and not to alter the position of slaves. This does not make him a bad person or a bad president. In his letter to Horace Greeley, he explicitly writes, "My paramount object in this struggle is to save the Union, and it is not either to save or destroy slavery. If I could save the Union without freeing any slave, I would do it."

Chapter 16 - The Presidency

"You say you will not fight to free negroes. Some of them seem willing to fight for you; but, no matter. Fight you, then exclusively to save the Union."

Abraham Lincoln, August 26, 1863

Lincoln's first course of business was to tour some of the states in the South. He stopped in Kansas in 1859 en route to other areas in the West. By early 1860, Lincoln made his second New England Speaking tour, although it didn't really start off that way. He was actually on his way up to the Philips Exeter Academy to see his eldest son, Robert Todd. Young Robert had just failed his entrance exams for Harvard, and Lincoln traveled to meet with him and offer courage and heart.

On his way, though, he decided to stop in New York to give a speech at the Cooper Union. That speech made such a big impact on the attendees that word spread of the content of the speech and of Lincoln's position. It was February 1860, and President Buchanan was in the White House.

As you can imagine, the speech revolved around slavery. The Cooper Union Speech was one that was based on an earlier speech that he had given at a church in Brooklyn, New York, some months earlier. Lincoln had done considerable research into extracting the intent of the Founding Fathers as to what their position would have been when it came to slavery.

He didn't need to look far.

The materials he had studied of the original signers of the Constitution showed that a slight majority had explicitly intended that slavery was not promoted in the Union. The rest, who were also against slavery, were not fully vocalizing their principles because they didn't want to offend their major donors, who were wealthy slaveholders. They agreed with the morality of the matter but had insufficient conviction to stand by it. Nonetheless, the original draft of Jefferson's Declaration of Independence explicitly made reference to the abolition of slavery. Lincoln had picked up on it and understood that the genetic makeup of America was not one that included slavery because it went against the core of American values of equality and freedom. To believe in the idea of America precludes participation in the institution of slavery.

What was lost on most people of the period and even today to a large extent is that America is not just a land sandwiched between two oceans. America is an ideal—a Utopian prototype that is significantly more intangible than it is tangible. It is more than its infrastructure, entertainment, and commerce. It is based on principles, practices, and pursuits instead of feudal patronage, vassalage, and enslavement.

It doesn't matter how much land is acquired or how we acquired it. It is not about how bravely we fight or how eloquently we energize our collective spirits, but the moment it is no longer based on ideals, it is no longer America. It is just a strip of land.

Among the founding ideals and principles, equity stands out as the basis of all else and strongly remains as the underlying current of all that is quintessentially American. Whether it is freedom of speech, religion, or assembly, whether it is the pursuit of happiness or the equal protection of the law, the thread that makes America America is equity.

During his years spent learning the law and then practicing it, he fell in love with the intellect and the compassion that characterized the framers, the Founding Fathers, and the deep thinking that was necessary to give birth to the nation. That is also the reason why he did not see the country as an extension of any practical religion. America was not born Christian. It was born free.

There were other facets of history that also prompted his position. He came to realize that when the Continental Congress met to debate and vote on the declaration the original draft that included the issues on slavery was part of the debate. It was decided during the debate to exclude the language on slavery because there were constituencies that were not willing to sign on to independence if it were included for the simple reason that slavery was allowed and in fact started by the British. It was something that bothered Jefferson.

The research that he had undertaken was to find the intent of the Founding Fathers and to seek guidance from the spirit of their intention. He found it, and it resonated with him that to be able to expound equity, and therefore freedom, supporting slavery would be untenable.

His long travels that took him across the states and territories, from the shores in the east to the plains in the west, gave him an opportunity to read and contemplate his findings.

On this particular trip to see his son, he was asked to stop in New York on the way and deliver a speech. By the time arrived to deliver the speech, the Young Men's Republican Union had decided to sponsor the event, increased the number of attendees, and moved the venue to cooper Union in Manhattan.

It was 1860, and Lincoln had not yet declared his intention to run for the presidency. Mrs. Lincoln was pushing the cause at home, and he was contemplating it on his travels. There were even rumors circulating that he might. The Young Men's Republican Union wanted to test his mettle and determine if they could find a candidate in this ex-congressman from Illinois, which is why they took over and sponsored the event. It was an audition of sorts, specifically by the New Yorkers so that they could understand his views, his character, and his abilities.

Most New Yorkers at this point had not seen or knew what he looked like. At first glance, it is widely reported that those who saw him thought very poorly of him. They had made the mistake of judging him from his awkward appearance. They were almost aghast at his appearance—lanky, too slender, and almost pale in complexion. He did not look presidential by any means, and they were collectively disappointed by his countenance.

In an illustration worthy of the phrase "do not judge the book by its cover," the room was spun on its head by the eloquence and intelligence of the man. The longer he stood there, the more he filled his suit and assumed the posture.

By the time he was a quarter of his way through the speech, the crowds were hooked on his every syllable. They were on their feet clapping, shouting, and asking for more. Every punctuation in his speech was met with explosive cheer and approval. The room was transformed as if by a spell that touched each heart and mind in attendance. They could no longer see the lanky and skinny "unpresidential" ex-congressman speaking. Instead, by the sound of his voice and the content of his mind, they saw a charismatic leader on fire before them. That fire of enthusiasm was infectious, spreading across the whole room and up that day and then in the days that followed up and down the Northeast corridor. It was the baptism of fire they needed to be converted, advancing him to the front of the line for the Republican nomination.

It will always be considered as the kindling that fired up the Republican Party.

"Who were our fathers that framed the Constitution? I suppose the 'thirty-nine' who signed the original instrument may be fairly called our fathers who framed that part of the present Government. It is almost exactly true to say they framed it, and it is altogether true to say they fairly represented the opinion and sentiment of the whole nation at that time. Their names, being familiar to nearly all, and accessible to quite all, need not now be repeated.

I take these 'thirty-nine,' for the present, as being 'our fathers who framed the Government under which we live.'

What is the question which, according to the text, those fathers understood just as well, and even better than we do now?

It is this: Does the proper division of local from federal authority, or anything in the Constitution, forbid our Federal Government to control as to slavery in our Federal Territories?

Upon this, Senator Douglas holds the affirmative, and Republicans the negative. This affirmation and denial form an issue; and this issue—this question—is precisely what the text declares our fathers understood "better than we."

Let us now inquire whether the 'thirty-nine,' or any of them, ever acted upon this question; and if they did, how they acted upon it—how they expressed that better understanding?

In 1784, three years before the Constitution—the United States then owning the Northwestern Territory, and no other, the Congress of the Confederation had before them the question of prohibiting slavery in that Territory; and four of the 'thirty-nine' who afterward framed the Constitution, were in that Congress, and voted on that question. Of these, Roger Sherman, Thomas Mifflin, and Hugh Williamson voted for the prohibition, thus showing that, in their understanding, no line dividing local from federal authority, nor anything else, properly forbade the Federal Government to control as to slavery in federal territory. The other of the four—James

McHenry—voted against the prohibition, showing that, for some cause, he thought it improper to vote for it.

In 1787, still before the Constitution, but while the Convention was in session framing it, and while the Northwestern Territory still was the only territory owned by the United States, the same question of prohibiting slavery in the territory again came before the Congress of the Confederation; and two more of the 'thirty-nine' who afterward signed the Constitution, were in that Congress, and voted on the question. They were William Blount and William Few; and they both voted for the prohibition—thus showing that, in their understanding, no line dividing local from federal authority, nor anything else, properly forbids the Federal Government to control as to slavery in Federal territory. This time the prohibition became a law, being part of what is now well known as the Ordinance of '87.

The question of federal control of slavery in the territories, seems not to have been directly before the Convention which framed the original

Constitution; and hence it is not recorded that the 'thirty-nine,' or any of them, while engaged on that instrument, expressed any opinion on that precise question.

In 1789, by the first Congress which sat under the Constitution, an act was passed to enforce the Ordinance of '87, including the prohibition of slavery in the Northwestern Territory. The bill for this act was reported by one of the 'thirty-nine,' Thomas Fitzsimmons, then a member of the House of Representatives from Pennsylvania. It went through all its stages without a word of opposition, and finally passed both branches without yeas and nays, which is equivalent to a unanimous passage. In this Congress there were sixteen of the thirty-nine fathers who framed the original Constitution. They were John Langdon, Nicholas Gilman, Wm. S. Johnson, Roger Sherman, Robert Morris, Thos. Fitzsimmons, William Few, Abraham Baldwin, Rufus King, William Paterson, George Clymer, Richard Bassett, George Read, Pierce Butler, Daniel Carroll, James Madison.

This shows that, in their understanding, no line dividing local from federal authority, nor anything in the Constitution, properly forbade Congress to prohibit slavery in the federal territory; else both their fidelity to correct principle, and their oath to support the Constitution, would have constrained them to oppose the prohibition.

Again, George Washington, another of the 'thirty-nine,' was then President of the United States, and, as such approved and signed the bill; thus completing its validity as a law, and thus showing that, in his understanding, no line dividing local from federal authority, nor anything in the Constitution, forbade the Federal Government, to control as to slavery in federal territory."

By the time he had left New York, word of his performance and his ideas had spread. Even though he was on his way to see his son, he ended up stopping a total of nine times along the way to repeat his message, each time to progressively larger crowds. He ended each speech to thunderous applause with these words,

"Wrong as we think slavery is, we can yet afford to let it alone where it is, because that much is due to the necessity arising from its actual presence in the nation; but can we, while our votes will prevent it, allow it to spread into the National Territories, and to overrun us here in these Free States? If our sense of duty forbids this, then let us stand by our duty, fearlessly and effectively. Let us be diverted by none of those sophistical contrivances wherewith we are so industriously plied and belabored—contrivances such as groping for some middle ground between the right and the wrong, vain as the search for a man who should be neither a living man nor a dead man—such as a policy of 'don't care' on a question about which all true men do care—such as Union appeals beseeching true Union men to yield to Disunionists, reversing the divine rule, and calling, not the sinners, but the righteous to repentance—such as invocations to Washington, imploring men to unsay what Washington said, and undo what Washington did."

Three things caught the attention of Northerners, Southerners, and the territories with this speech.

1. The first, obviously, was that the Constitution was not promoting slavery in its intention. He proved that the individual signers were not intending slavery by virtue of their past behavior and their silence on various bills that they were involved in crafting and voting on. By that he enforced the idea that the Union was never intended to bless the idea of slavery.

2. The second, and this is more important but often missed, is that he was exerting the federal government's power over the states. This was almost more concerning than the issue of slavery.

3. The third, and this was related to the issue of slavery, was that he truly saw those that looked different from him as equals. After two hundred and fifty years of being around slaves and lording over them, many had forgotten that those they called slaves were human and deserved equality.

For those who were listening to the speech, its content resonated perfectly to the way the North had evolved since '76. The South had gone one way and the North the other. In time, it was two worlds driven apart by unique climate profiles, which drove unique industries and advancements, which drove unique self-preservation issues. The South grew dependent on the slave population, while the North did not.

The crowds he stood before proved insatiable. They wanted to bask in the glow of his words and understand the content of his character. They had caught a glimpse of both that afternoon at the Cooper Union. He energized their imagination and animated their involvement in the crusade against the expansion of slavery into the new territories. In return, their enthusiasm empowered him with the confidence he needed to push forward toward his destiny and to overcome whatever his hesitation was to make the decision.

By the time he arrived at Exeter Academy, word of his speeches at the nine stops along the way from New York had traveled far and wide at the speed of wildfires during an Indian summer. It had also made its way down south to fall on the ears of staunch Southerners and slaveholders, wealthy and poor alike.

While the North jumped in jubilation, the South winced at what was being contemplated and what that implied. They were not strangers to abolitionists or their talking points, but this was different. This time there was a conviction in the heart and tenacity at the lips of the chief proponent. What's worse was that he was right. The Founding Fathers and the framers of the Constitution did not envision slavery. The South had grown used to the forbidden fruit, and now it was almost impossible to consider a world where there was no slaves.

After visiting Robert, his solitary time on the long journey back was spent in contemplation of a presidential run. Word was out by that point that he would have to go up against Stephen Douglas, his old nemesis, if he were to enter the race.

Based on his eventual writings and thoughts chronicled by those around him at the time, it is clear that he was suspended in the chasm of indecision for some length of time. On the positive side, he was encouraged by the crowds that cheered him and his wife who motivated him. In his own mind, he had a duty to the country to set it on the course of righteousness.

On the other side of the chasm was the darkest of voices within him that feared the process, feared losing, and feared the penetrating daylight of a national campaign.

Even though Lincoln had done well in previous contests, it was only because of his personal charm—as seen during his speech at the Cooper Union in Manhattan. It was the same when he won his seat in Congress—by meeting almost everyone in the district and charming them with his eloquence and calm. That would, however, be impossible to replicate across the country. It would not be possible to meet every single constituent for a national contest the same way it had been in those district contests. Lincoln understood this limitation.

He also knew that his position on a number of things, as morally and legally accurate as they were, were not popular positions in a large part of the South. It would be almost impossible to get any traction in the South. Stephen Douglas was significantly more popular and more presidential. He also had policies that app

Another aspect of Lincoln's decision was based on who was behind him in the effort. He would not have been able to pull off a nomination much less the election if it were not for a grassroots effort, which had to be orchestrated, and only the new Republican Party was able to pull that off.

During the Republican Convention that year, which was held in Chicago between May 16 and May 18, 1860, the favorite to gain the nomination was Senator William Seward. Lincoln's last-minute nomination was a surprise to all but a few supporters. His Cooper Speech had catapulted him to the front of the line. Even his surprise entry at the last minute was able to garner the support necessary to become the nominee.

All this was not just because of his speeches and growing popularity but also because of a highly able and witty campaign manager, who steered the strategy from before Lincoln had made the decision.

Behind the scenes, a lot of horse trading followed the planning. Lincoln had agreed to give out Cabinet positions and keep Hamlin as his vice president.

There is a misunderstanding of what the Republican Party stood for, especially in today's context. Even the word "Republican" is rooted in the word "republic" and stands for a central federation. The Republican Party of Lincoln's day was liberal (as much as it could be in the mid-nineteenth century). Conversely, the Democratic Party, which Steven Douglas belonged to, was the conservative party of the day.

The core push of the Republicans back then was for a centralized system of governance. They believed that the efficacy of being one nation rather than a grouping of states loosely brought together was more efficient and would be stronger. But the solution brought with it other problems. It also meant that the states would no longer be able to control their own destiny, which was something that had been fought long and hard for just a century earlier.

The Republican Party was not looking at it from the perspective of the consolidation of power but from the fact that there were shared interests that could be combined to provide better economies of scale. Think about the military today, where its budget is greater than the combined budget of two dozen of the largest military forces in the world. That kind of economies of scale could not be achieved if the states had chosen to keep control over their own military and not have one national defense complex.

In the same vein, there were other shared issues that provided greater utility than standing individually. The Republicans, under Lincoln, saw this as the driving force of their endeavor, but this would not sell in the North, the South, or anywhere else in the young country at the time. The one thing that all the states were united on was that states' rights were paramount within a federal context.

There is a countervailing argument to the states' rights issue that rose in the antebellum period. The first was not entirely honest, and that was that the South was actually more interested in having a stronger federal government. Alternative historians argue that it was in the best interest of the South that the federal government was stronger so that they could enforce the rights of the Southern states to have runaway slaves that escaped to the North to be returned to them. This is an argument that makes no sense whatsoever. This argument is not disputing the states' rights argument; instead, it is confusing states' rights with enforcement of one state's law in another.

With this out of the way, it is clearer to see what the path of using slavery as a proxy war would be. There was also the fact that the South was trying to weaken the hold of the federal government because it was electorally disadvantaged. In the years leading up to the Civil War, there were more antislavery congressmen thane pro-slavery congressmen by virtue of population distribution. The South had a smaller population and an even smaller voting constituency since millions of slaves that were in the South didn't vote.

Population density gave the Northern states more say in who would be president and the advantage in distributions in Congress necessary to pass legislation.

The issue of slavery would then become the key to advancing the benefits of Republicanism (in this case, mending central government control).

The Republicans represented the notion that being one country was better than being what is merely a union of states, and for that they needed to bring the country closer together. This was a view that at the time was controversial and not reflective of the reality at the grassroots level.

That changed over time, and today the Republican Party is no longer the party of Lincoln. It is the party of conservatism. There is certainly nothing wrong with that. It just goes to show that the values Lincoln championed should not be confused as being conservative. As history clearly shows, they were liberal. It has just become convenient for the present crop of Republican politicians to brand themselves as the party of Lincoln.

Lincoln's goal as president was to champion the legislation to abolish slavery and return the United States to its righteous path. It was also to build the mind-set of one nation rather than a federation of states. In a twist of fate and a case of "be careful what you wish for," he got both when the South declared that if the Republicans won, they would secede from the Union.

Another matter that escapes public awareness is that presidents under the system of the U.S. government do not have structural control over legislation. That still sits with the legislative branch of government. The president's job is to enforce the laws that are already on the books and advance the country within those laws in a way that he sees fit.

Strong presidents have pushed members of their party to prioritize their agenda and election promises. Sometimes that has worked; sometimes that has backfired. In an alternate history, if the South had not seceded and the country had not plunged into a civil war, it would be difficult to see how it would have been to legislate what Lincoln envisioned.

The rest, as they say, is history. From there Lincoln went on to win the general election that year in part because he was a good candidate standing up for a strong cause that lit the base. More importantly, though, the reason why he beat Stephen Douglas is simply because the Democratic Party had split that year, and the vote split between him and John Breckenridge. That allowed Lincoln to win the electoral votes and ascend to the presidency.

Chapter 17 - Lincoln's War

Lincoln's whole life was a war filled with battles at every point of consequence. He had to battle for everything he never acquired or wanted. He had to battle for the women he loved, do his job, and to learn. If war was his life and battle was his way, then strength of mind was his artillery. His strength of mind was legendary but often not spoken of in great detail.

Lincoln's battles were not something most people could have fought much less won the way he did. His strength came from his weakness. We have seen that weakness in the chapter on his spiritual center and other areas of the book.

The critical aspect of his time in office was derailed because of the secession of the South. Had that not happened, Lincoln had other plans for his legacy. The main push behind Lincoln's presidency would not have been to abolish slavery in the South but to prevent the new territories from coming in as slave states. Lincoln did not intend to abolish slavery because that would upset the apple cart too much.

Lincoln wanted to quickly expand to the west and advance the revenue of the nation to build the infrastructure in the East and North. For that he needed the country to be a powerful tax base, and for that he could not have abolished slavery.

To be clear, he did not support the indignity of slavery. He supported industry and a strong tax base, which, in turn, was driven by slavery. Before secession he never insisted that the South stop slavery, but they did not like the idea of the new states not to be slave states.

In the Republican Party, there was the notion that even the South should be free from slaves. Lincoln was not part of this platform. When he took on Andrew Johnson as his running mate in 1864, the battle between him and his previous vice president, Hannibal Hamlin, was exactly about this issue. Hamlin wanted to push the South into becoming free. What made it work out the way it did was because a war had already started, and the war took precedence over the freeing of slaves or any other matter.

Chapter 18 - Second Term

For most of the Civil War that began just three weeks after his inauguration and lasted until a few days before he was assassinated, it was a war that initially seemed righteous. But as the bodies began piling up beyond the imagination a country can afford, people began to turn on the efforts of Lincoln. By June of 1863, Lincoln was faced with a tactical and political conundrum.

If he failed, not only would slavery have become commonplace all across the Union, but his efforts to alter the course of history would be forever lost, and his belief that he was meant to do great things would be a lie he told himself. The cost of failure was too high for the country, for the office of the presidency, and for his own mind. Those factors and the possible consequences powered him through his sleepless nights, but with Mrs. Lincoln steadfastly behind him, he leaned into the wind.

From a factual standpoint, the tides had turned at Gettysburg in 1863 and at Vicksburg the same year. If it hadn't happened, Lincoln's approval rating would have been permanently damaged. Before the victories, those in his own party were already gunning for him, and he was despised by even his own generals, who were referring to him in rude and uncomplimentary terms.

Until this point in his presidency and this juncture in the war, Lincoln had been too acquiescent to those whom he thought knew more than he did. He knew what needed to be done but didn't have the strength to do it because the will of this decisions was less than the full measure needed. Lincoln had the resources to end the war the first year, but because of his hesitance and his unwillingness to rely on his own counsel, the North wasted time, resources, and lives.

Each president is the manifestation of the times they serve in. That is the power of a democracy and something that is not fully understood by the masses. The presidential election, if not aided by nefarious external forces, is the sum aggregate of the will of the people. In all the things he says and all the things they perceive in him, and in the troubles that plague the country, he is the manifestation of the solution. It is up to him to use the apparatus of the other branches of government, whether to bring them together, to persuade them, or to veto them, in taking action that is in the best interest of the country.

But to do that, Lincoln had to take full control of the powers that were available to him and to come into himself in the decision that he had to make. Since nothing happens overnight, it took time for him to cascade into a position that allowed him to have full confidence in himself, his assessment, and his solutions.

All he needed was a shift in the way he perceived himself. The question that lies in every one's mind is the events that result in this fortunate shift. It wasn't good prevailing over evil. Lincoln's fortunes didn't turn because he was right. They turned because Lincoln, it turns out, was a master tactician.

What changed was Lincoln's self-assessment and governing style. Up to the spring of 1863, Lincoln was a passive commander in chief, which allowed his generals to run roughshod over him. Generals do not have the benefit of the overall view. They only see areas that they are in charge of. Lincoln had been relying heavily on their input, and he was not inserting his ideas and strategies into the discussions. In fact, in many of the battles they had lost, he realized that his initial instincts and ideas were right, but he had deferred to the generals, and they had instituted it without the full perspective he had. Lincoln's secretary, who was in attendance in all the meetings and taking notes, wrote that Lincoln would give in to the generals' "whims and complaints and shortcomings as a mother would indulge her baby." It had reached such a critical point that those generals stopped respecting and adhering to Lincoln's "timid" suggestions. In the summer that year, all that changed.

The shift in demeanor preceded the shift in strategy. He no longer nudged them or made a suggestion. Instead, he gave them strict instructions, and if they didn't follow them down to the last-minute detail, they were fired. He took charge in sweeping fashion, and the generals snapped straight with respect. Within a month from the time he snapped out of his passive ways, the country started to see a difference in the outcomes of the battles. That one last shift, on his part, altered the trajectory of the war, the composition of the United States, the state of slavery, and the history that might have been. *The New York Times*, which had been relentlessly criticizing Lincoln until now fell in line and was singing his praises. As goes *The New York Times*, so goes the North.

The presidency and the war taught Lincoln a major lesson. Even when you take feedback and suggestions, the final decision is the commander in chief's. As one of his later successors famously said, "The buck stops here." Lincoln had figured that out himself, and the tide had decisively changed.

It couldn't have come at a better time. The tide had turned just as the presidential election of

1864 was coming around. Whatever dissension that existed within the party over the direction of the war had been tamped down, but the issue with slavery still remained as a source of tension between Lincoln and Hamlin so much so that Lincoln decided to pull Andrew Johnson and excluded Hamlin.

By this point, the Republican Party had temporarily altered their name and called themselves the National Union Party. Lincoln had some competition for the nomination, but after the war turned around, he beat any competitor who would stand in his way.

He went on to win the general election, which was held in November 1864, for a second term in 1864 with 55 percent of the popular vote. He carried twenty-two out of twenty-five states that voted that year and accumulated 212 electoral votes.

There was a change in his demeanor and in his outlook. The confidence of his own abilities, which had eluded him and compounded by the depression that he had grown to accept as part of his inner self, had been shattered. Many people who saw Lincoln in the waning days of the war saw a man reborn.

After the reelection, Lincoln went back to the business of running the country and making plans to rebuild. He was prompted to punish the South on many occasions during the war, and he was once again heavily lobbied to do so. Lincoln was resolute in his declination.

The postwar reconstruction of the South and the North to a much lesser degree was always on Lincoln's mind even from the earliest days of the war. Now the time had come, the formal surrender was imminent, and the thoughts of reconciliation filled his mind to a greater degree.

He knew that imposing reparations and penalties would not be a wise solution. The North and South were after all part of one family. Instead, Lincoln saw fit to forget and forgive and alter the course of history by unifying the country and to strengthen the bond between the federal government and the states. It was at this point that he, as part of the reconstruction and reunification, imposed that all states had to abide by the federal antislavery laws. By doing that, he officially elevated the United States of America into the light of freedom for all.

On the afternoon of April 9, 1865, General Robert E Lee surrendered to General Ulysses Grant at Appomattox Court House. The two generals had engaged in battle that morning, but when it was clear to General Lee that his options were nonexistent and that he had been cut off from retreat, he surrendered.

The surrender documents were concluded, and a ceremony to disband was instantly executed with men in the Confederate army returning their weapons before being freed to return to their homes. The Confederate army was disbanded. Lincoln had won the war, and all of the country, North and South celebrated. The celebration was more in the North, but the South was happy that the killing was over with. When it was all said and done, more than 600,000 men died in the line of duty fighting their brothers. It was the most brutal war America had experienced. In comparison, American casualties in World War II were 420,000.

Chapter 19 - John Wilkes Booth

John Wilkes Booth was a bastard, and that is meant literally. His father eventually married his mother only on John's thirteenth birthday. Booth's father, Junius Brutus Booth, was part of a family of popular stage actors who settled in the Baltimore area. Merely saying they were popular really doesn't cut it. They were the leading family name in all of theater and known by high society of the Northeast Corridor stretching from Boston to Washington, D.C. and even down in to Virginia.

Junius Booth was as eccentric as he was popular and was the period's most well-known and well-thought-of Shakespearean thespian. Edwin, John's older brother, was also an accomplished actor in his father's footsteps. John Wilkes, however, was initially a dud when he tried his hand at acting. He didn't have the background and the depth of knowledge that stage actors who took on Shakespeare's plays needed.

His youth was one of privilege in terms of the way he was raised on a large farm and with few things to care about. His youth was as different from Lincoln's childhood as night contrasts day. His family farm was in Bel Air, Maryland, which sits almost exactly halfway between Philadelphia and Washington, D.C.

The Booth clan was as liberal as could be in their politics and most decidedly on the side of the North when the Civil War eventually broke out. All of them were staunchly of the North except John Wilkes. On this matter, he would have severe arguments with his family and was the outcast when it came to this subject.

The patriarch of the Booth clan was a dyed-in-the-wool thespian who represented the intellectual side of the art, while John Wilkes had no such streak. But he was ambitious. He wanted to be as good as his father and certainly better than his older brothers. His ability, at first, fell short of his goals. Even though he was fluent in the language, he couldn't deliver the nuances that riddled the plays he was cast in, and the nuances couldn't fly.

Then he found something that neither his father nor his brothers could offer that he could. It turned out that John was nimble and energetic and brought a very powerful action sequence to the stage, which was something that the audience had not experienced, and he started getting acclaim for this. Even though his popularity rose everywhere in the county, it gained the most in Virginia.

John was indeed handsome and full of energy. He became an instant hit on the stages of Virginia once he started bringing action to his character, and he was, in fact, the first actor in America to be so attractive to the women audience that his clothes were ripped away one day as he walked through the crowd.

He repaid this glowing adulation by staying in the South for consecutively longer stretches of time and slowly began to understand their concerns and favor their politics. Before long he was fully sympathetic to the Southern plight and began to be resentful of the Northern perspective.

As his popularity grew, so did his affinity to the South. As his affinity to the South grew, the more it divided him from his family and increased his hatred toward a president who was taking the country in a new direction by virtue of his policies.

When the unknown Lincoln began campaigning for the presidency, the South had started to dislike what they had been hearing, and when he ascended to the presidency and it seemed that he was able to put his campaign rhetoric to practice, the states in the South that hadn't supported him began fomenting the idea to secede from the Union.

It was around this time that John Wilkes began despising Lincoln and could not bring himself to see an America that Lincoln saw. His hatred grew so deeply that more than once when he was on stage at Ford's Theatre and President Lincoln was in attendance, he would direct fiery speeches or scenes that were part of the play while looking directly at Lincoln. This happened often enough that caused Lincoln to comment a couple of times that he felt Booth was directing some kind of animosity toward him.

It has been constantly studied by scholars that the final act of the assassination would not have been possible if it not for a confluence of events. What started out as an idea to kidnap Lincoln then advanced to the notion of assassinating him because of Booth's state of mind and the events that were happening in the war. The war had ended, and the South had lost, sealing the notion of slavery in the South and shaking Booth to his core. Compounding that was the failure of his oil well in the North that had rendered him broke. If he had waited a few weeks, his other oil well would have begun producing, and he would have been wealthy. We may be reading about him instead of Rockefeller, but his exasperation in his personal life, his loss on the political front, and his hatred of a man who was everything that he was not leading the country put Booth into a mind-set that altered the course of American history.

Booth on his own was not a bad person. Who among us has not made mistakes that we later regret? We regret these mistakes because in the heat of the moment we commit mistakes resulting from poor decisions, which prevent us from seeing the true nature of our actions and their eventual consequences. Booth was no different. In his mind, he had lost everything, and the idea of losing the South of which he was so attached altered his sense of right and wrong. In no way are we trying to justify what he did to be acceptable or right. Regardless of one's politics or the losses we incur in our pursuits does it give us the right to take a life, president or pauper.

Chapter 20 - Last Act

"Now he belongs to the ages"

Edwin Stanton, April 15, 1865

Two days after the surrender at Appomattox, Lincoln delivered a speech, which stresses that his focus would be the reconstruction of the Union, both in the North and the South. America was united again, and he was the president for all, North and South. John Wiles Booth was in the audience listening to the speech as he seethed with hatred and disappointment. At the end of the speech, Booth, who as you will recall had intended to kidnap Lincoln during the war, now advanced his conspiracy and declared, "Now, by God, I'll put him through. That is the last speech he will ever make."

On the evening of April 14, 1865, shortly after 10:00 p.m. while the play was under way, Booth entered the upper-level box that the president and First Lady occupied. At the same time, it was planned that Vice President Andrew Johnson was to be assassinated as well, but Booth's accomplice, George Atzerodt, who was supposed to do the deed, backed out. The other member of Lincoln's cabinet who was to be killed that night was Secretary of State William Seward. He was stabbed, and although he survived, he was brutally disfigured from the wounds to his face. The man who attacked him, Lewis Powell, was hanged for his crimes.

Back at Ford's Theatre, as the Lincolns were in a celebratory mood, Lincoln reached over and held his wife's hand, which in those days was not what polite society did in public. But it was a romantic gesture. Mrs. Lincoln smiled and wondered aloud to her husband what their friends would say if seen to which Lincoln replied in a whisper, "*She wouldn't think anything about it.*" As he said this, Lincoln, who was in an extremely good mood, was listening to the play and laughing at a comedic line delivered by Harry Hawk. In that instant, as Lincoln held his wife's hand, the theatre was shaken by the loud noise of the .44 caliber Derringer pistol that discharged the single bullet that lodged in Lincoln's frontal lobe after entering behind his left ear and shattering his orbital plates. He slipped into a coma with Mary Lincoln sobbing uncontrollably by his side.

Soldiers carried Lincoln's comatose body in the rain to a house across the street and up to the first-floor bedroom. Doctors arrived and could see that even though Lincoln was still alive the gunshot was fatal. Lincoln's oldest son arrived less than two hours later and found his father unconscious but breathing peacefully. There was no suffering in the final moments of his death. He was at peace. There were no convulsions and no sounds. By 7:00 a.m. the next morning, it looked more like he was soundly and peacefully asleep. At 7.22 a.m. on April 15, 1865, President Abraham Lincoln passed on to the ages.

Conclusion

We need heroes in our life so that we can aspire to the better angels that they aspired to. It is not about hero worship or a reason to adulate at the feet of a myth. These achievers need to be seen as they are—faults as well as virtues. Only then can their achievements be an example for the rest of us.

This applies to President Abraham Lincoln, the sixteenth President of the United States. Born on April 12, 1809, to an upstanding family under harsh conditions, he grew up in one frontier land after the other until he finally settled down, early in his youth, in Illinois. He had decided to take responsibility for his own fate and to be the cause of his lot in life.

That fate turned out to be something that no one he grew up with would have ever come to expect. Even for Lincoln himself, he did not aim for higher office until after he left the U.S. House of

Representatives after one term. He came to realize that as a congressman, one of many, he was unable to make change or to move the country in any way. Toward the end of his term, he realized that he needed to do more. He had considered the Senate and then the presidency.

Out of the forty-five presidents who have held the office, Lincoln holds the honor of being the only one to oversee a civil war and be the cause of almost half the country attempting secession. Whether he caused the chain of events that led to that or he perpetuated the war by his lackluster performance in the early part of the conflict is not the point of this book. Nor should it be the point of any analysis of Lincoln.

Analyzing Lincoln with the aim of learning from his strengths and identifying the weaknesses one could avoid requires that his life be seen under the light of truth and respect. Lincoln was by all means a regular man and one who was fallible in many ways. He had to live with the visage of one that was not always appealing to others, and that determined the path of his life from his teenage years.

Yet, he persevered. He began to drop his reliance on how he looked to something he could change, which is what he knew. Beyond that he looked to become part of a culture of industry. In other words, he wanted to use his resources of work and stamina to be able to make a name for himself. He did.

The first lesson that anyone could ever hope to extract from his life would be that regardless of where one is born or under what conditions they are born into, there is always a way to climb out of it. We live in a world today that has cultivated obesity and poverty at the same time because we have done away with self-discipline and self-reliance.

Lincoln's life is the antithesis of today's mind-set. He used his mind to think about the big things, and that made him the giant in his days whose shadow was cast onto ours. The widow of the late Martin Luther King once said that "small men cannot do big things." This applied, in reverse, to Abraham Lincoln. He was a big man who was able to do big things.

The Romans have a saying, which roughly translated means, "to conquer the world, one has to conquer his own self." In other words, one has to be able to conquer his own thoughts, his own demons, and his own sins before he can go on to do big things. Lincoln was a big man who could conquer his own mind and go on to do truly great things.

Lincoln had a number of tools to help him in this effort. He found that reading helped, and within the practice of reading, he found that memorizing lines helped take it further. It is one of the reasons why he associated learning and memorization with happiness and intelligence. Over the course of his adult life, he memorized quotes, passages, and entire poems almost effortlessly, and this brought peace and clarity to his soul.

Lincoln's psyche and persona is his own, but it did build on the example and psychology of his father. When Lincoln lost his sister and his mother, he was young and did not know how to react to the catastrophe. Children who are still psychologically developing base their responses to stimuli on the adults who are responding to the same stimuli as well. Lincoln watched his father for clues on how to react to things that happened around them and to them.

What he found was that his father harbored deep depression, stemming from his trauma as a child himself. When death visited the Lincoln household repeatedly, it brought with it a dark cloud to settle over Lincoln Senior. It injected silence into his demeanor and incapacitated the man of the house. For Lincoln Junior, the death of his mother unexpectedly robbed him of both parents, not one. With his mother gone and his father retreating into depression, he was left to grapple with the pain of childhood and the grief of loss without the benefit of a soothing voice or cuddling arms. It was fortunate that Sarah was there for him even though she was not much older than he was, and she was facing the same pain. The siblings grew closer from this shared loss and the unfortunate state of affairs.

Lincoln's depression and melancholy were not just from the events that shaped his life. Those were bad enough to trigger his depression, but the fact that helped it along and aggravated it was that he was also thought to deal with problems in a way that was inverted. The saving grace for him was that he had taken up a pastime that his father had not—reading.

In the course of his reading, he learned to elevate the way he spoke and the way he thought. This overlapped with rules and ultimately the law that society had to operate under. This was of profound interest to him. Law gave him the structure that family and religion could not. Once he began to understand the concept of law and the way societies organized themselves, he elevated his views and started questioning the ways humanity organized itself, and he turned to the Roman books of history. He started to understand the value of freedom and the power of democracy. However, he also saw some of its shortcomings.

In understanding those shortcomings and the latent weakness, he came to appreciate the need for power and unilateral decisions. He began to see the true nature of the presidency. Whether or not the Founding Fathers felt that it was to be used in such a way was another point altogether, but to him it was a stroke of genius.

There have been a few presidents in the history of the United States who have been such a force of will themselves that they single-handedly expanded the power of the presidency and the reach of the office. It was never intended for a king to rule this country and to demand adulation from his subjects. Instead, the country was built to be governed by itself. Be that as it may, the Office of the President, while created by Articles of the U.S. Constitution, does have tremendous latitude in its development, and that gave a handful of men the ability to expand its role.

George Washington, as much as he did for the nation in the Revolutionary War, was not such a president who could expand on the powers of the presidency during his tenure and neither were men such as Jefferson or Adams. Only two men in our history have expanded the powers of the presidency and pushed the bounds of the office. Abraham Lincoln was one of those men.

Historians have been debating the legality and righteousness of the actions of men like Lincoln who have tried to expand those powers. Some have labeled those who have succeeded as usurpers, while others have regaled them as presidential and carved their visage into mountains. Regardless of what men think after the fact, none of them can ever imagine or emulate the intensity of the mind that carries a man from the backwoods of the frontier to the hallowed halls of the White House.

www.ingramcontent.com/pod-product-compliance
Lightning Source LLC
Chambersburg PA
CBHW030147100526
44592CB00009B/158